Lesson Study

ALSO AVAILABLE FROM BLOOMSBURY

Special Educational Needs: A New Look (2nd edition), Mary Warnock and Brahm Norwich, edited by Lorella Terzi

Effective Teaching and Learning in Practice, Don Skinner

Lesson Study

Making a difference to teaching pupils with learning difficulties

EDITED BY BRAHM NORWICH AND JEFF JONES

BLOOMSBURY
NEW DELHI • LONDON • OXFORD • NEW YORK • SYDNEY

First published in India 2018
First published 2012

Bloomsbury Academic India
An imprint of Bloomsbury Publishing Plc
BLOOMSBURY, Bloomsbury Academic India and the Diana logo are trademarks of Bloomsbury Publishing Plc

This edition published with permission from Bloomsbury Publishing Plc,
50 Bedford Square, London, WC1B3DP, UK

British Library Cataloguing-in-Publication Data
A catalogue record for this book is available from the British Library.

Library of Congress Cataloging-in-Publication Data
Lesson study : making a difference to teaching pupils with learning difficulties /
edited by Jeff Jones, Brahm Norwich.
pages cm
Includes bibliographical references and index.
ISBN 978-1-78093-576-8 (hardback) — ISBN 978-1-78093-830-1 (paperback) —
ISBN 978-1-78093-740-3 (epdf) 1. Special education—Great Britain.
2. Lesson planning—-Great Britain. I. Jones, Jeff, 1950- II. Norwich, Brahm. LC3986.G7L47 2014
371.9—dc23
2013031530

ISBN 978 93 88002455
10 9 8 7 6 5 4 3 2 1
For sale in the Indian subcontinent only
Bloomsbury Publishing India Pvt. Ltd
Second Floor, Building No.4
DDA Complex LSC, Pocket C - 6 & 7
Vasant Kunj, New Delhi 110070
www.bloomsbury.com

Typeset by RefineCatch Limited, Bungay, Suffolk
Digitally Printed and bound in India by Replika Press Pvt. Ltd.

Contents

Acknowledgements

We would like to acknowledge the help and support given to us in writing this book. In particular, we would like to thank:

The Esmee Fairbairn Foundation for its generosity and to Derek Bardelow for his guidance.

Hilary Hodgson who made the project possible when she worked at the Esmee Fairbairn Foundation.

Professor Charles Desforges, Emeritus Professor, University of Exeter.

Abigail Patterson, Project Officer (formerly), Graduate School of Education.

Staff and students from the schools who participated in the Lesson Study-MLD project and agreed to contribute to the research.

Jacqui Pennington, Jill Wright, Philippa Steadman, Susan Tilstone, Kathy Dobbie, James Harrison, Jane West, Marie Barrett, Debbie Burman, Lee Jackson and Susie Eden whose Lesson Study cases are reported in Chapters 4 and 5.

Notes on contributors

Peter Dudley is often seen as the person who has introduced Lesson Study to the UK. He ran the national Lesson Study pilot from 2003–5. This was a cross-phase project funded by the Economic and Social Research Council (ESRC) Teaching and Learning Research Programme, the National College for School Leadership and CfBT. Pete has conducted extensive research on Lesson Study at the University of Cambridge, UK, and promoted professional learning through Lesson Study throughout his four years as National Director of the Primary National Strategies. He has written practical guides for teachers and schools leaders and provided advice to policy makers. Pete is supporting Lesson Study research programmes at the University of Exeter, UK, Queens University Belfast, UK, and the University of Cambridge, UK. Pete set up the 'What Works Well' classroom practice transfer website and has overseen the creation and training of over 1000 leading teachers who use Lesson Study approaches to help colleagues to improve practice in other schools. Pete's international work with Lesson Study has been in Singapore, Hong Kong, Chile and the US. He is an active council member of the World Association of Lesson Studies. He has been Assistant Director within a UK Local Authority from July 2011.

Ruth Gwernan-Jones is a Research Fellow at the Graduate School of Education, University of Exeter, UK. Her areas of speciality include special educational needs, particularly specific learning difficulties, and disability studies. For her Ph.D. she documented the experience of being dyslexic with dyslexic adults, looking at the meaning 'dyslexia' had for them and focusing on the ways in which they developed self-perceptions and coping skills.

Di Hatchett is an independent education consultant and Director of the Every Child a Chance Trust, a charity formed and funded by the business community in order to develop robustly evidenced approaches to early intervention. Now available nationally, the Trust's programmes: *Every Child a Reader* and *Every Child Counts* provide successful school improvement models for raising the achievement in literacy and numeracy of children falling into the lowest 20 per cent of attainment in primary schools. Di's career in primary education has spanned over 40 years and includes 12 years as headteacher of a large urban primary school and a period as a senior local authority manager. Prior to joining the Trust, Di was Senior Director within the previous government's National Strategies, responsible for its cross phase work on inclusion and intervention for all children at risk of under-achievement. She now acts as a professional adviser to a number of projects and initiatives related to improving the progress and life chances of struggling learners.

Jeff Jones (co-editor) is an independent consultant. He was a Principal Consultant with CfBT Education Trust, working in the UK and overseas. While at CfBT, he participated extensively in the design, delivery and quality assurance of national training programmes; in research and evaluation projects; and in a variety of leadership and management consultancies. Previously he had been Principal Lecturer at a University School of Education, where he was responsible for the coordination of research and for continuing professional development (CPD). Before that, he was a member of a large local authority inspection and advisory team. At various times during that time he was responsible for pupil assessment, appraisal, management and professional development, as well as for governor services. He has researched and published extensively in the areas of continuing professional development, school leadership and management development, performance management and school governance. His most recent research projects include one on the role of chairs of school governing bodies with a team from the University of Bath, UK, and a second, with a team from the University of Exeter, UK, that investigates the impact of Lesson Study on pupils with moderate learning difficulties.

Gill Jordan is a well-known national exponent of Lesson Study, has carried out her own research lessons, and helped others to do so in schools. She has presented on Lesson Study at numerous National Strategies literacy events and conferences. She is a member of the World Association of Lesson Studies (WALS). She used to be a senior member of the National Strategies literacy team and is responsible for the development of guided writing pedagogy amongst many other things. She spent several years teaching in Hong Kong. She is also a reading recovery leader.

Brahm Norwich (co-editor) is Professor of Educational Psychology and Special Educational Needs at the Graduate School of Education, University of Exeter, UK. He has worked as a teacher and as a professional educational psychologist and has researched and published widely in these fields. His previous books include *Moderate learning difficulties and the future of inclusion* (Routledge, 2005); *Special pedagogy for special children: pedagogies for inclusion* (with Ann Lewis, Open University Press, 2005); *Dilemmas* *of difference, disability and inclusion: international perspectives* (Routledge, 2008) and *SEN: a new look* (Continuum, 2010) (with Mary Warnock and Lorella Terzi).

Annamari Ylonen is currently a research fellow at the Graduate School of Education, University of Exeter, UK. She previously worked as a research fellow in the area of widening participation in higher education at the University of Greenwich, UK. Her publications include various academic articles and a book *Specialisation within the Finnish comprehensive school system: reasons and outcomes and equality of opportunity* (VDM Verlag Dr. Muller, 2009).

PART ONE

Introduction

The first section of the book aims to explain what is meant by Lesson Study, how it has come to prominence and the contribution it stands to make to the learning of pupils generally, and to pupils with learning difficulties in particular. It also describes the development and outcomes of the development and research project undertaken by a team from the Graduate School of Education at the University of Exeter that investigated the impact of LS on the teaching and learning of pupils with Moderate Learning Difficulties (MLD). The first chapter by Brahm Norwich and Jeff Jones introduces Lesson Study, outlines its relevance to inclusive teaching of pupils with learning difficulties and summarizes the Lesson Study-Moderate Learning Difficulties project. In the second chapter Pete Dudley explains the rationale and underlying principles of Lesson Study and suggests reasons for its use by teachers of children with MLD. In the third chapter Ruth Gwernan-Jones examines the background and contemporary ideas and research about moderate learning difficulties and pedagogic issues in teaching pupils with MLD.

1

An Introduction to Lesson Study: Its Relevance to Inclusive Teaching of Pupils with Learning Difficulties

Brahm Norwich and Jeff Jones

Introduction

Our aim in writing this book is to explain how the principles of Lesson Study work in practice for children and young people with learning difficulties, its distinctive features compared to other collaborative developmental techniques, and to offer examples from schools in the UK of its successful use by teachers in both primary and secondary schools.

The book presents an account of Lesson Study's varied use, with particular reference to a recent development and research project at the University of Exeter that focused on secondary school teaching of pupils with moderate learning difficulties (MLD) across a range of curriculum areas. Lesson Study case studies are used to highlight teachers' experiences of applying a Lesson Study approach to address varied pedagogic themes and questions and capture how teachers develop more inclusive teaching strategies for pupils with learning difficulties, especially those with MLD.

Lesson Study is a powerful development strategy that has its origins in Japan and has also been used internationally in Singapore, Hong Kong and the USA for many years, but less so in the UK. The key role of shared planning, teaching and assessing to improve practice was highlighted in an international review of school systems that were assessed as the most improved by the consultants McKinsey (Barber *et al.*, 2010). Lesson Study represents just such an approach. However, its use has been mainly in the professional and teaching developments in specific subject areas, e.g. mathematics education (Hart *et al.*, 2011). Although Lesson Study can be used in different phases and areas of education and with a focus on different pupil characteristics, we have found no references to its previous use in developing inclusive teaching of pupils with special educational needs or disabilities in ordinary schools.

In Singapore, Chia and Kee (2010) have adopted a version of Lesson Study in the training of special education teachers who teach in separate classes and schools, but not for general class teachers. Also, although there is a tradition of inquiry-based approaches to inclusive school and teaching developments (Ainscow, 2000; Miles and Ainscow, 2011; Howes *et al.*, 2009), these approaches have not used Lesson Study practices. We chose Lesson Study as a general teaching development approach because of its previous international record of promoting pedagogic knowledge and strategies. In particular, the UK version of Lesson Study, with its focus on particular pupils' learning (Dudley, 2004), had specific relevance to the teaching of pupils with identified special educational needs (SEN) or disabilities as part of general class teaching (see Chapter 2 for more details).

The main themes and issues dealt with in the book are:

1. the theory, practical uses and benefits of Lesson Study for pupil learning, with reference to pupils with learning difficulties;
2. how Lesson Study works in practice in different areas and phases of schooling; and
3. how Lesson Study can promote developments in areas of class teaching that continue to challenge practitioners, such as meeting the needs of pupils with learning difficulties.

In this introductory chapter, we discuss the concept of MLD as used in the UK, and explain why the focus is on this aspect of SEN. We then examine Lesson Study in more detail to show how it is relevant to developing the teaching of pupils with learning difficulties. This leads to a brief outline of the development and research project – *Raising levels of achievement through lesson development for pupils with moderate learning difficulties* – on which the contributors to the book collaborated as a team. The project will be called the Lesson Study-MLD project in this book. We conclude with an outline of the chapters to follow in the rest of the book.

Moderate learning difficulties

While pupils with MLD represent the largest proportion (23 per cent) of all those identified as having special educational needs in the English school system, they have tended to be neglected as a focus for educational initiatives.

(Chapter 3 has more details of the relative proportion of identified pupils with SEN.) Another way to represent the incidence of identified MLD is that 2 per cent of all pupils in the English school system in 2010 (about 168,000 pupils) were identified as having MLD at School Action plus or Statement levels (see below for details of these levels). This compares with the 8.6 per cent of all pupils identified at these levels as having a SEN (DFE, 2011b). The neglect of this group can be attributed to several factors. Pupils identified with MLD come disproportionately from families who experience socio-economic disadvantage compared to other areas of SEN, such as autism, and speech and language impairment. There has also been no well-established advocacy or voluntary group dedicated to the interests of these pupils in this country.

Part of the neglect of the education of pupils with MLD comes from the uncertainties and contention about the educational definition of MLD. This is partly about whether the category refers to general low attainment (very low attaining) or whether it involves both general low attainment and low general intellectual or cognitive functioning, as indicated by low general cognitive abilities, as measured by cognitive ability or IQ tests in the score range of 50/55–70 (Norwich and Kelly, 2005). The Department for Education and Skills (DfES) definition of MLD refers to 'much greater difficulty than their peers in acquiring basic literacy and numeracy skills and in understanding concepts' (DfES, 2003), but the phrase 'and in understanding concepts' is unclear as to whether this means low cognitive abilities and, if so, how low? However, there is no doubt in the Government's definition that MLD is regarded as a form of SEN.

This means that there will be different pupils identified as having MLD depending on how the term is understood and used. In the English SEN system, at the point of writing this book, there are three levels of special educational needs: 1. School Action; 2. School Action plus; 3. Statement. (Legislation is going through Parliament to reduce this to two levels – 1. School Action; 2. Education, Health and Care Plan). There is also a decreasing rate of identification from School Action to the Statement level. The area of SEN is also only recorded at the more significant levels of SEN, School Action plus and Statement. Table 1.1 shows recent data about the number of pupils at these two levels and in ordinary or special schools.

Table 1.1 shows that just under half of all pupils identified with MLD at the most significant level (Statement of SEN) are in primary and secondary schools, with the rest in special schools. Those with Statements and in special schools are also likely to have lower levels of attainment and have more associated difficulties (e.g. social skills, emotional and language difficulties) than those with Statements in ordinary schools (Norwich and Kelly, 2005). The table also shows that those with Statements are a minority (23 per cent) of the total identified as having MLD in the annual census; most are in ordinary

Table 1.1 Breakdown of percentage of English pupils with MLD by level and placement in 2012 (DfE, 2012b)

Identified with MLD	School action plus	Statement	
Primary schools	65,930	6,390	
Secondary schools	48,790	10,895	
Total in ordinary schools		17,285	49%
Special schools		17,430	51%
Total overall	114,720	34,715	
	(77%)	(23%)	

schools (77 per cent), which is where the Lesson Study-MLD project was mostly focused. However, the figures above do not represent pupils identified at School Action (11 per cent), who make up about half of all those currently identified as having SEN (21 per cent).

The difficulties of pupils with MLD – like all those with SEN – do not fit neatly into single categories. Though the above figures represent pupils' main area of difficulties, they are likely to have other associated difficulties.

Table 1.2 shows one scheme that involves two dimensions, the degree of learning difficulties (i.e. difficulties in acquiring literacy, numeracy and understanding concepts) and whether these difficulties are associated with other difficulties. The background history and context of the use of the MLD term will be examined in more depth in Chapter 3.

Table 1.2 A scheme for defining MLD

Associated with	Milder learning difficulties	More severe learning difficulties
No other significant difficulties		
Significant emotional and behavioural difficulties		
Significant sensory and / or medical difficulties		

Based on Crowther *et al.*, 1998.

Lesson Study

This book aims to show that Lesson Study, as a classroom-based professional development approach, has considerable relevance to and potential for teaching pupils with MLD. High-quality and effective Lesson Studies have been characterized as practices that 'help teachers enhance their content knowledge and pedagogical content knowledge to improve instruction in classrooms, develop good "eyes" to see and analyse student learning, and ultimately to produce better student learning' (Yoshida, 2012: 141). Existing research about the mechanisms and outcomes of the process indicates, for example, that Lesson Study improves teaching by developing teachers' knowledge, by building professional community among teachers, and by improving teaching materials (Lewis, 2009). This, in turn, can have a positive impact on pupil learning. Research has also shown that the collaborative aspects of participating in Lesson Study through the planning and review meetings can enhance teacher efficacy, which can lead to improved engagement and learning of pupils (Puchner and Taylor, 2006), and that teachers can acquire new insights into teaching and how to improve their teaching strategies via participating in Lesson Study (Lee, 2008; Rock and Wilson, 2005). There is also evidence of the development of effective learning communities in schools that have engaged in a longer-term Lesson Study process (Lieberman, 2009).

Lesson Study encourages teachers to develop their own agenda for enquiry, using searching questions about their lesson planning and teaching in terms of learners' learning outcomes. Lesson Study involves a small number of teachers (3–5 usually) collaborating over the planning, teaching and reviewing of specific lessons. In doing so, these teachers, and others supporting pupils' learning, e.g. specialist teachers and teaching assistants, adopt a research mode which focuses their review and planning on 1–3 'case pupils' that are representative of the selected theme. These teachers also draw on their professional knowledge and relevant professional and research-informed knowledge about their focus to jointly plan, observe and analyse the case pupils' learning. They capture and refine the developing practice through the use of video and audio recordings, and find ways of helping others by sharing with peers what has been learned. This is the version of Lesson Study written about in this book and used in the Lesson Study-MLD project (see Figure 1.1). This reflects a UK version of Lesson Study that will be examined in more detail in Chapter 2.

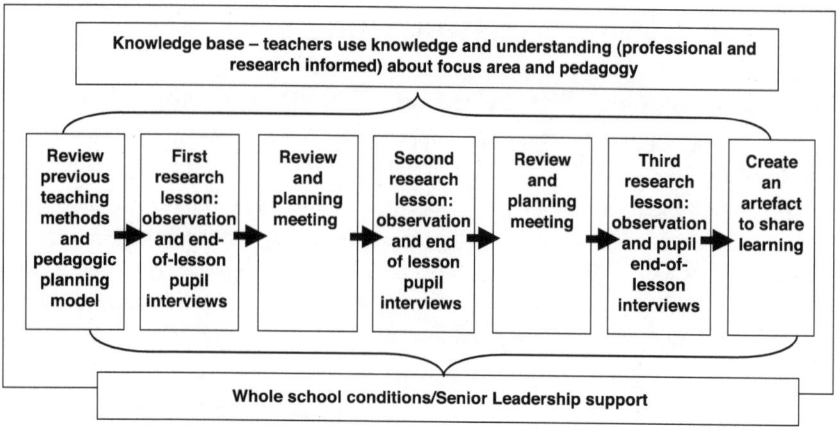

Figure 1.1 *Model of Lesson Study used*

The Lesson Study-moderate learning difficulties project

Teaching pupils identified with MLD is a challenging and neglected area of special needs and inclusive education and is complicated because it involves important questions about the boundaries between SEN and non-SEN. This is a particularly topical issue in England following Ofsted's (the national school inspection agency) recent national review of SEN (Ofsted, 2010), which concluded that too many pupils are identified as having SEN. This position was then adopted by the current Coalition Government in its planned legislation that is going through parliament at the time of writing. This will mean that pupils currently identified as at School Action (11.3 per cent), which is just over half the total number identified (19.3 per cent; DfE, 2012b), will no longer be identified as having SEN. Primary and secondary class teachers will then be expected to teach them as part of the spectrum of pupils with below average and lower attaining pupils.

As we would expect from the uncertainties about the term MLD, as discussed above, and as will be shown in detail in Chapter 6, the term MLD is used in very variable ways. Some identified as having MLD may just have below average attainment but do not meet the difficulties 'in understanding concepts' criterion. Because there have been difficulties in distinguishing MLD from those with below average attainments, we have opted to use the term '*learning difficulties*' to refer to this spectrum of difficulties in learning that range from MLD to below average attainments and that crosses the SEN–non-SEN boundary. As shown in Chapter 6 on the evaluation of the

Lesson Study-MLD project, the book addresses these issues of teaching and learning for those pupils across the spectrum from MLD to low attainment. This focus is therefore timely and relevant for the changes implied in the new English SEN legislation.

The Lesson Study-MLD project also has to be seen in the context of a recent development in English schools that is relevant to MLD. This is the Government's 'Achievement for All' initiative following the Lamb Enquiry (DCSF, 2009), which was a unique attempt to raise the aspirations and achievement of pupils with SEN and disabilities with a focus on educational outcomes. Achievement for All was a large-scale multilevel project covering 10 local authorities and 450 schools. Its outcomes have also been very positively evaluated (DfE, 2011b) leading to its interventions being adopted by a national charity to disseminate the approaches to schools. One of its three main strands was about assessment, tracking and teaching interventions. Though we understand that there was some small-scale use of Lesson Study as part of this strand, most of this intervention was at a whole-class level and did not have the well-defined professional development focus and protocols of the Lesson Study-MLD project.

The Lesson Study-MLD project, with its focus on key stage 3 (11–14-year-old pupils) within secondary schools, was based at the Graduate School of Education, University of Exeter, and funded by the Esmee Fairbairn Foundation. The two central aims of the project were to:

- enhance the achievement of MLD pupils at Key Stage 3 (ages 11–14 years); and
- develop pedagogic strategies, programmes and materials for wider national use in secondary schools.

These aims were elaborated into seven specific project aims:

- to make a significant national contribution to secondary school provision for pupils with MLD;
- to develop pedagogic knowledge and strategies, programmes and materials for improving the learning and learning dispositions of pupils with MLD for wider national use;
- to enhance the professional development of participating teachers (development and research knowledge and skills, pedagogic strategies relevant to pupils with MLD and pupils in general);
- to enhance curriculum and pedagogic development and the self-development capacity in participating schools;

- to evaluate the processes and outcomes of the Lesson Study development work;
- to evaluate the usefulness of the MLD category; and
- to disseminate the findings and products of the project in a way that has a significant national and international impact.

We approached these aims by having two interrelated wings, a development and an evaluation/research wing (see Figure 1.2). The development wing was responsible for implementing and adapting lesson teaching using the Lesson Study methodology, while the evaluation wing provided external monitoring and evaluation. This design exemplified what has been called a Development and Research model (D&R), an approach to innovation, knowledge creation and dissemination (Bentley and Gillinson, 2007). This design moves away from the dominance of the traditional R&D model that depends on the application of research into practice. The D&R model is more grounded in the needs of teachers and pupils and is flexible and teacher-oriented.

The design of the project can also be understood in terms of the distinction between two routes to researching school teaching improvements: a *general proof route* and a *local proof route* (Lewis *et al.*, 2006). The general route (R&D) starts by establishing causal efficacy claims and then disseminates with an emphasis on fidelity of implementation. However, controls to ensure fidelity can lead to restricted local buy-in, and adoption may not occur when central controls are no longer there. By contrast, in the local proof route, innovation is local and may differ across settings, but there can be continuous adaptations, local ownership, early adoption and the organic spread of the innovation. However, local conditions might result in adaptations that undermine the potential of the innovation, while knowledge about the innovation may be local and tacit. Also, as the data to improve innovations are local, general efficacy claims are likely to be weaker. Lewis *et al.* (2006)

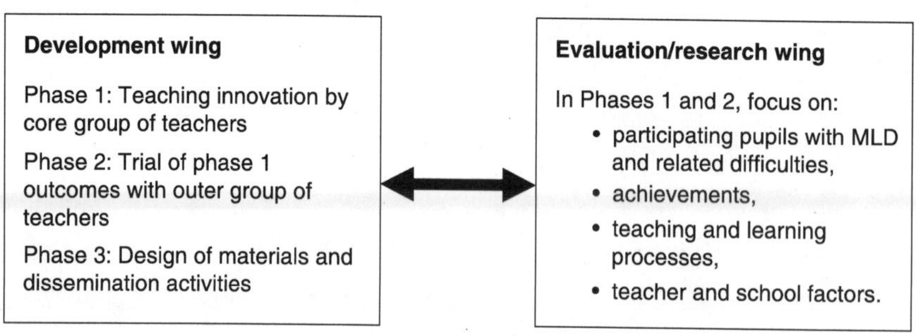

Figure 1.2 *Design of the project*

suggest that there is a trade-off between these two proof routes, with each having advantages and disadvantages. Though the general proof route may be strong on internal validity (that is, to identify causal efficacy and an intervention) it may be less so on external validity (that is, the relevance of the demonstration to use in other settings, other subject areas and learners). These disadvantages are often overlooked. This does not imply that general route proof designs cannot or should not be used in Lesson Study research, only that so far they have not because Lesson Study is still mainly a development strategy rather than a specific method or intervention.

So, this project adopted a local route proof approach as Lesson Study was at an early stage, needing to be defined in operational terms. We judged that a general proof route with the use of randomized controlled trials (RCT), was more suited to well-defined interventions where the intervention is less likely to interact with the context of its use. Another way of seeing the design of the project was therefore as design-based research (Cobb *et al.*, 2003), where the project evaluation would refine the use of Lesson Study; so providing evidence from the particular use of Lesson Study to develop teaching approaches for pupils identified as having MLD.

The project's main focus on literacy and the arts/humanities in Key Stage 3 had a number of reasons. Literacy is arguably the most important outcome for schooling. Literacy teaching for pupils with MLD has not had the same degree of attention as literacy has had for the majority of pupils who do not have these learning difficulties. Linking literacy and the arts/humanities curricula could also create rich possibilities to promote the use of literacy skills in meaningful and enjoyable ways. There were two main reasons for the focus on Key Stage 3 secondary school pupils. Key Stage 3 has been associated with a well-established dip in pupils' rates of progress (especially among pupils with learning difficulties) that can threaten their longer-term motivation to learn. Another reason was that Lesson Study had not been tried on this scale in secondary schools; the previous Lesson Study project had been in primary schools (NCSL, 2005).

Phase 1

Schools in four local authorities in the south-west of England were contacted directly and through the University of Exeter School Partnership about taking part in the project. These were two urban authorities and two county authorities. The secondary schools had between 750 and 2000 pupils with most around the 1000 pupil level. Each school had two teachers to lead the Lesson Study work; they attended the project training and review conferences and involved a few other colleagues in their Lesson Studies. Although 18 schools signed up to the project and attended the initial one-day preparation conference, 14 completed the Lesson Study cycles (due to staff illness, maternity leave and other work commitments). Out of the 14 schools, 3 were special schools that were included to compare how Lesson Study worked in smaller classes that only had pupils with SEN.

Participating teachers became initially involved in the Lesson Study in different ways. In some schools, teachers were informed about the invitation to become involved, and senior teachers encouraged, or at least did not block, those who showed an interest. In others, interested teachers were asked to apply and a senior teacher decided which teachers would take part. A senior manager in each participating school signed a memo of understanding with the project team about mutual responsibilities over the period of the project. Funds were provided to schools to cover teacher release from their class teaching for the initial, interim and final Lesson Study day conferences for all project schools and to have time to undertake the school-based review and planning meetings required in the Lesson Study approach. Schools were also loaned video recording equipment to record aspects of research lessons, and, once started, a project consultant supported Lesson Study teams through visits and/or phone contact. Schools also agreed to become involved in the evaluation research.

The participating teachers, who taught pupils in Key Stage 3 (11–13 years old), were expected to be from different subject areas to enable cross-curriculum collaboration. The main subjects represented were English, humanities and/or art, though there were a few in the mathematics/science area. These teachers also recruited other Lesson Study team members in their schools who could include senior teachers (e.g. deputy head teachers), Special Educational Needs Co-ordinators (SENCOs) (the lead teacher in each school with responsibilities for coordinating provision for pupils with special educational needs), teachers from other departments, teaching assistants and trainee teachers. All of the secondary school teachers in phases 1 and 2 of the programme had previously taught pupils identified as having MLD as part of their general subject classes. The participating teachers had to identify 1–2 pupils as the case pupils, aged 11–13 years, who had been identified as having MLD, as the focus for the Lesson Study process. The teachers were also expected to liaise with the SEN coordinator to ensure that those pupils identified were recorded as having MLD in the school met the national definition of MLD (DfES, 2003).

The Lesson Study team membership in the 14 schools varied between 2 and 5 or more per school, with 5 schools only having 2 members and the majority of schools (9) having 3 or more members. Lesson Studies were conducted in a range of classes including pupils of mixed attainment well as lower attainment-grouped classes. The special school classes were smaller than ordinary school classes. Of the 28 teachers, 82 per cent were female and 18 per cent were male, about 90 per cent were aged under 40, and about 60 per cent of the teachers had less than 10 years of teaching experience, while the remaining 40 per cent had been teaching for over 10 years.

Phase 2

As will be explained in Chapter 6, the evaluation wing evaluated the phase 1 Lesson Study processes and outcomes. Lesson Study procedures were adapted for phase 2 in several ways on the basis of this evaluation. It was decided to introduce a more focused way of setting learning goals for case pupils in the phase 2 design of the Lesson Study procedure because teachers in phase 1 tended to report outcomes in generalized ways. Not only would this help the Lesson Study teachers plan their research lessons in terms of more focused learning goals, but this would also provide a way of monitoring pupil learning and outcomes for the phase 2. This system is explained in detail in Chapter 6.

The outcomes of Lesson Studies for schools were also shown to be less positive and more mixed than for Lesson Study pupil and teacher outcomes. There were a number of problematic aspects about the organizational conditions of Lesson Study practice that emerged from this analysis, despite the positive aspects of the Lesson Study process and funding to pay for teacher cover. Specific issues were about the timetabling of meetings, arranging teacher cover and sometimes teachers using their free time to undertake the Lesson Studies. Another issue was related to senior leader support for Lesson Study, in some but not all participating schools. In view of these experiences, it was decided to focus more attention on the senior leaders of the phase 2 schools to persuade them to become more interested and find better ways of releasing teachers to undertake the Lesson Studies, as explained below.

In the second phase, there were 33 teachers from 15 secondary schools from the same local authorities but three were from the south-east of England and three were special schools. They had a similar introduction conference as phase 1 teachers and operated in similar ways to phase 1. All schools completed the Lesson Study programme phase. However, the teachers in the second phase received less guidance and support while undertaking the Lesson Study process in order to determine how Lesson Study would operate under conditions more similar to those typical in schools. The Lesson Study team membership varied between two and five or more per school: 1 school had 2 members, while the majority (12) had 3 or more members (data missing for 2 schools). Of the 33 teachers, 80 per cent were female and 20 per cent were male; 90 per cent were aged less than 40 years old; while 36 per cent had less than 10 years of teaching experience and 64 per cent had more than 10 years of teaching experience.

Concluding comments

We have explained in this introductory chapter how the Lesson Study-MLD project brought together an aspect of professional learning/school improvement (Lesson Study) with an area of special needs and inclusive education (teaching pupils with MLD). This interaction was also reflected in the composition of the Lesson Study teams to be cross-curricula and cross-role. This book reflects a similar collaboration of colleagues in the project team from different areas of education and with different backgrounds and roles.

The organization of the book

The book is organized into three sections. This introductory chapter (Chapter 1) has started off Part 1. In the next chapter (Chapter 2) within this section, Dr Pete Dudley sets out the general rationale and underlying principles of Lesson Study. Chapter 3 is by Dr Ruth Gwernan-Jones who examines issues about the MLD category and pedagogy for pupils in the MLD-low attainment spectrum. Part 2 contains two chapters that examine case studies of Lesson Studies in practice. In Chapter 4, Gill Jordan draws on Lesson Studies across the country that involved pupils with learning difficulties to show how Lesson Study operates at the primary school phase. Di Hatchett, in Chapter 5, outlines some case studies from the Lesson Study-MLD project in secondary schools. There are two chapters in Part 3 of the book. In Chapter 6, Dr Annamari Ylonen and Professor Brahm Norwich summarize the lessons from the evaluation of the Project Lesson Studies. In Chapter 7 Dr Jeff Jones and Professor Brahm Norwich outline the future prospects and ways forward, with conclusions and recommendations.

2

The General Rationale and Underlying Principles of Lesson Study

Pete Dudley

Introduction

Much mainstream and special school-based teaching of pupils with learning difficulties is excellent. There are reasons why some teaching of these pupils is less than good. The teaching may suffer from poorly constructed assessments of need, by practice that is informed more by misplaced, even stereotyped teacher expectations of students' capabilities and motivations than informed by a sound understanding of how the particular pupil can best learn and be supported to learn.

Such situations can arise as a result of assumptions that are held by teachers about the nature of the learners purely because of the specific 'special educational needs' (SEN) label that has been attached to them. These assumptions can lead to teaching that is poorly 'pitched'. If a teacher does not fully understand the barriers through which a pupil with learning difficulties needs to be supported then the learning may be pitched at too high a level. If a teacher has subliminally 'categorized' the pupil as having 'SEN', they may automatically lower the pitch inappropriately, resulting in learning that is unchallenging for the pupil. This can happen when there is over-dependence in a school on a curricular intervention or teaching scheme for children with special education needs, but which may still be poorly matched to the very different specific needs of particular learners. These three traps – (1) poor assessment of learning need, (2) use of teaching interventions that do not necessarily meet needs, and (3) allowing deterministic assumptions to lower expectations of student's capabilities – can all contribute significantly to poor-quality teaching of children with MLD and therefore to their success as learners. Any approach that helps schools and teachers to avoid these traps must therefore be worthy of exploration.

The processes and outcomes of the Lesson Study-MLD Development and Research project reported on in this book explored the use of a Japanese approach to the development of professional knowledge and learning for teachers who were teaching secondary-aged pupils with MLD in mainstream and special schools. (A fuller definition and explanation of MLD is provided in the previous and the next chapters.) This professional learning model is called Lesson Study. The project sought to establish whether Lesson Study might offer an approach that helps schools to avoid falling into some of the common traps described above.

Indeed, Lesson Study has been identified as a key contributor to the deep knowledge that Japanese teachers seem to maintain and develop throughout their careers of their subject and curriculum, of their pedagogy and of their pupils themselves. Furthermore, Japan has maintained some of the highest educational standards worldwide, despite experiencing a sustained economic downturn. The use of Lesson Study by over 900 leading teachers in the UK National Strategies was also linked with increases in pupil attainment (Hadfield *et al.*, 2011; Dudley, 2012).

Evidence from a pilot of Lesson Study developed in England by the author (Dudley, 2005, 2008), as well as a growing bank of international evidence (Stigler and Hiebert, 1999; Willis, 2002), suggests that what distinguishes Lesson Study from other models of professional learning is that it focuses almost exclusively on the learning of specific pupils and how this learning can be improved, rather than focusing on teaching, teaching techniques or teachers. Lesson Study seemed to offer the Lesson Study-MLD project an approach that has been demonstrated to:

- help teachers to develop their ability to see their pupils *with fresh eyes* (Dudley, 2007 see below);
- help teachers to be able to discern these pupils' learning needs more clearly and accurately;
- develop much better understanding of factors that can constitute barriers to their learning (barriers that may be presented by the curriculum they are being taught or pedagogical approaches that are being used to teach it, but also by cultural and logistical aspects of the mainstream or special school classroom-learning contexts in which these pupils were learning); and
- develop ways of overcoming these barriers.

The big question for the Lesson Study-MLD project was to find out whether Lesson Study could help to develop 'deep knowledge' about the needs, expectations and support for the learning of pupils with MLD in very different classrooms – both mainstream and special school.

The first section of this chapter gives an overview of what Lesson Study is. It explores each component part of the Lesson Study process and highlights those elements that might prove to be valuable in its use by teachers of children with learning difficulties.

The third section of the chapter suggests how a UK adaption of Lesson Study contains two distinctive elements that I developed in the Lesson Study project. Evidence from my work in the research and development of Lesson Study suggested that the use of *case pupils* and the involvement of pupils in the process could be particularly important elements to include in the Lesson Study-MLD programme.

Much professional development – including that which aims to tackle issues such as determinism and teacher expectation – frequently fails to change teachers' practices in the long term. So, in the third section of this chapter, I will summarize evidence from the literature on the characteristics of professional development that most impact on classroom practice and pupil learning and test Lesson Study against this evidence. I conclude that engaging teachers in collaborative enquiries into improving pupils' learning can change their beliefs about what pupils with MLD are capable of learning and can also provide practical ways of helping teachers to provide support for that learning to be achieved.

Brief introduction to Lesson Study

Lesson Study is a form of collaborative classroom enquiry in which a group of teachers work together to improve their pupils' learning by improving the way they teach aspects of the curriculum, knowledge or skills, or the ways in which they develop their students as learners and citizens. The process evolved in Japan and has been practised there since the 1870s. Lesson Study is instantly recognizable to teachers in the UK as a form of action research. However, the models of action research upon which much UK classroom enquiry has traditionally been founded (Elliott, 1991; Carr and Kemmis, 1986), were originally developed by Lewin in the 1940s. Japanese Lesson Study had already been around for 70 plus years even then. However, because it was mainly recorded and communicated on a local basis by serving teachers for use by other teachers, and because this was nearly always in Japanese, knowledge about Lesson Study did not travel outside of Japan until the late 1990s. American researchers identified it to be a key component in Japan's resilient, high-performing school system and to be a contributing factor to the deep knowledge that Japanese teachers possess and maintain of their curriculum subject and of their learners' needs (Lewis, 1998; Stigler and Herbert, 1999).

Lesson Study has the following five components (Dudley 2011: 9):

1. Identifying themes and groups for improvement;
2. Formulating hypotheses and goals – the Lesson Study focus;
3. Joint research lesson planning, observation (and elicitation of pupil feedback);
4. Post-research lesson discussion, analysis and initial planning for the next research lesson (there will usually be three or so research lessons); and
5. Passing on the knowledge gained in the Lesson Study to others.

Identifying themes and groups

Most Japanese teachers are members of at least one Lesson Study group at any point throughout their careers (Watanabe, 2002) and some may belong to several at once. In England and other countries where Lesson Study is not part of the historic fabric of school routine, Lesson Study groups are chosen by school leaders who need to be able to create opportunities for them to work together on the five components of Lesson Study.

Before any Lesson Study group sets to work, it is important that the group has established some protocols to govern the way in which they work together. This is especially important if the group is new or if members of the group are new to Lesson Study. The protocol should make it clear that whatever their usual roles within the school or beyond, when they are involved in the Lesson Study they:

- are all equal;
- are all learners;
- are committed to learning from each other's contributions (irrespective of the seniority or experience of the people involved); and
- all share a common goal – which is to build knowledge together from each individual's store of knowledge about teaching and learning and also from the knowledge they collectively build while planning, observing, comparing perspectives and analysing the ways their pupils are learning in the research lessons.

A clear set of protocols governing the way the Lesson Study group should operate makes it easier for the individual members of the group to develop trust with others and to build the social capital that the group needs in order to function well. Protocols can help overcome individuals' feelings of vulnerability caused by planning and teaching in close proximity with colleagues. It encourages people to take risks, to try out new approaches and to venture ideas and challenges without fear of criticism.

Establishing the Lesson Study focus

Lesson Study group members review the teaching, learning and achievement of pupils in their classrooms, school or department and decide upon an area for improvement that becomes the focus of their Lesson Study. They then carry out research into the agreed area of focus, seeking out what evidence there is of curricular or pedagogical approaches that make a difference to pupil learning and development in their area of focus. They may draw upon the experience and knowledge of local subject experts, university professors, local authority (in Japan 'prefecture') advisers or members of Lesson Study groups in other schools or departments who have experienced success in improving learning in a similar area of focus.

Joint research lesson planning and observation

Once the focus is established and some initial research has been done, the group will come together in order to plan their first classroom enquiry in which they will try to put the research into action in a scheduled classroom lesson. These classroom enquiry lessons are called research lessons.

The group plans the first research lesson collaboratively before one of them goes on to teach it, while the other group members carry out a carefully planned observation of the ways in which pupils learn (and do not learn) in the research lesson.

During this lesson planning process the group defines very carefully what it hopes the pupils will be able to do, understand or know by the end of the research lesson. They will usually plan the lesson in a number of phases – again focusing on how they hope the pupils will progress during each stage of the lesson – that should combine to create the overall gains planned for the pupils by the end of the research lesson. They plan carefully to use the specific approach or technique that they discovered through their initial research and which they are committed to trying out in the research lesson in order to better meet their pupils' needs. They will usually need to articulate and agree what the intended progress of the pupils in the various stages of the research lesson will look like – what the pupils will be doing or will have accomplished in terms of their work if the intended learning is going to plan. This process of 'joint imagining' (Dudley, 2011) and recording of the intended learning they are designing in the research lesson, holds the Lesson Study group members to account for their expectations of the progress of their pupils. This is because it provides the group with a detailed, agreed and recorded hypothesis for what should be observable amongst the students if the research lesson is going to plan in terms of the learning it is generating.

The joint research lesson plan then becomes the prompt sheet for the observation of the research lesson by those group members who are the observers. Observers annotate the lesson plan as they observe what actually

Research lesson planning, observation and discussion sheet Subject, Learning Focus Teacher/observer

What this research lesson is aiming to teach (it may be a section of a longer teaching sequence) **What teaching technique is the research lesson aiming to develop?** ***We are improving...***							
Current attainment and success criteria Describe what you are looking for from them by end of lesson in the identified aspect	Case pupil A .... **Success criterion for this focus**		Case pupil B .... **Success criterion for this focus**		Case pupil C .... **Success criterion for this focus**		
Stage of lesson sequence	How you hope case pupil(s) A will respond	*How they are observed to respond*	How you hope case pupil(s) B will respond	*How they are observed to respond*	How you hope case pupil(s) C will respond	*How they are observed to respond*	Patterns /issues
Stage ... (approximate time)							
Stage ... (approximate time)							
Final stage ... (approximate time)							
What were they able to do? (What progress have they made and how do you know?)							
Initial thoughts							

Figure 2.1 *Research lesson planning template*

Source: NCSL (2005).

happens in terms of the pupils' learning, compared with the learning the group had predicted would happen.

The role of the post-research lesson pupil interview, which has become a feature of Lesson Study in the UK along with the use of case pupils, will be explained in the next section.

Post-research lesson discussion

At the end of the research lesson the Lesson Study team meets to analyse the pupil learning behaviours that they observed in the research lesson. They bring together their evidence – annotated lesson plans from the research lesson observations, examples of pupils' work, and pupil feedback on the research lesson (provided through post-lesson interviews – see the section below). Of course, where the post-lesson discussion can take place immediately after the research lesson, they bring – still fresh in their minds – the snapshots of key moments, snatched lines of dialogue or critical pupil and teacher exchanges that occurred during the lesson. These are key to the quality of the analysis that the Lesson Study group can carry out and many of these ephemeral details fade and are lost in only a few hours – so a prompt post-lesson discussion is essential.

Classrooms are amongst the most complex and fast-moving work environments that exist. Elsewhere (Dudley 2011, 2013), I have reported extensively on the way that the pooling of multiple perspectives of what happens in a research lesson not only slows down the lesson's action (Gallimore and Stigler, 2003), but also allows far more to be seen in relation to the ways that specific pupils learn in the research lesson. For example, errors in teachers' assessments of pupils' needs are frequently discovered. Such discoveries can radically change the ways in which these pupils' learning is planned for in the future.

Takahashi (2005) has outlined important elements that make the post-lesson discussion productive. These include the need to base comments and hypotheses on observed evidence. He also stresses the value that can be added by a member of the Lesson Study group acting as chair of the discussion, and he gives examples of the value that can be added on occasions by the presence of an expert member who joins the Lesson Study group and who can contribute significantly to the quality and insightfulness of the discussions. Work in this country with leading teachers (Hadfield *et al.*, 2011) supports this view.

One feature of the post-lesson discussion developed in my Lesson Study pilot and subsequent work is adherence to a 'post-lesson discussion information flow' (Dudley, 2008). This flow goes from learning to teaching, as shown in the sequence below:

1. Observations of case pupils.
2. Questions and discussions about the way other pupils learned.
3. Questions and discussion about the data on the teaching.

Adherence to this flow can help to root the Lesson Study group's discussion in the evidence gathered from observations and pupils' work. This keeps the focus of the discussion on the learning of the pupils, before it begins to become speculative about the reasons why the particular learning was or was not observed and the way that the *teaching* affected this. Lesson Study group members have repeatedly stated (Dudley, 2011) that staving off the discussion about the teaching until a later point is key to facilitating teacher learning, because it focuses attention away from the teacher. They also say that this reinforces the feeling that the teaching was collectively planned by the group, and that if it did not have the desired effect at any point the responsibility for that rests with the group and not with the one member of the group who happened to teach the lesson on the group's behalf.

'What is very powerful is that people felt that because they'd planned it together, it made it okay if it went wrong' (Lesson Study Pilot teacher, in Dudley, 2012: 91).

This feels very different from the judgemental feedback teachers frequently experience through performance management or inspection and which, they report, tends to stifle rather than promote risk-taking and teacher learning.

As the key findings of the post-lesson discussion emerge and are recorded, the Lesson Study group inevitably begins to plan elements of the next research lesson. In this planning they will tweak aspects of the lesson that they have just analysed, in the hope that they can help pupils to learn even more effectively. I stated earlier that Lesson Study can be understood as a form of action research. One thing that distinguishes Lesson Study from action research, however, is the fact that every Lesson Study and every research lesson always have broadly the same research question: 'How can we teach X more effectively to Y?'

A Lesson Study group will usually teach three or four research lessons, each one refining and tweaking their approach until the group believes that it has established some new practice knowledge that could be used again by themselves in their own classrooms and by others in similar situations.

Passing on the knowledge gained in the Lesson Study to others

At this point the Lesson Study group turns its attention to recording what it has been learning and the difference that this newly developed knowledge can make to pupils' learning. Teachers in Japan take the passing on of knowledge to others as a serious professional duty. As stated above, they write and publish brief Lesson Study reports, which are widely read by Japanese teachers. And they do more. They invite colleagues to attend a lesson in which one of the group will use the new approach. These events are called 'open house' research lessons. When knowledge has been developed that is felt to have very wide potential application and effect, the Lesson Study group teachers may be invited to hold a 'public research lesson'. This builds on the Chinese tradition of public teaching. In a public research lesson, a class of pupils will be set up in a hall and an invited audience of local teachers, advisers and academics will observe the lesson being taught – including the modelling of the new approach – in the round. Following the public lesson there is a discussion involving the audience members, Lesson Study group members and the pupils about the merits and applications of the public research lesson.

In the next section of this chapter, I will go into more detail about the importance of this part of the Lesson Study process, a part that is often the least well-practised in this country. Figure 2.2 illustrates the model of Lesson Study described above and adopted for use by the Lesson Study-MLD project. This final knowledge-sharing stage is represented by the 'create an artefact' rectangle.

As Figure 2.2 shows, the whole process of planning, teaching/observing, and analysing the sequence of three research lessons combined with the process of disseminating the knowledge gained, is what constitutes one Lesson Study.

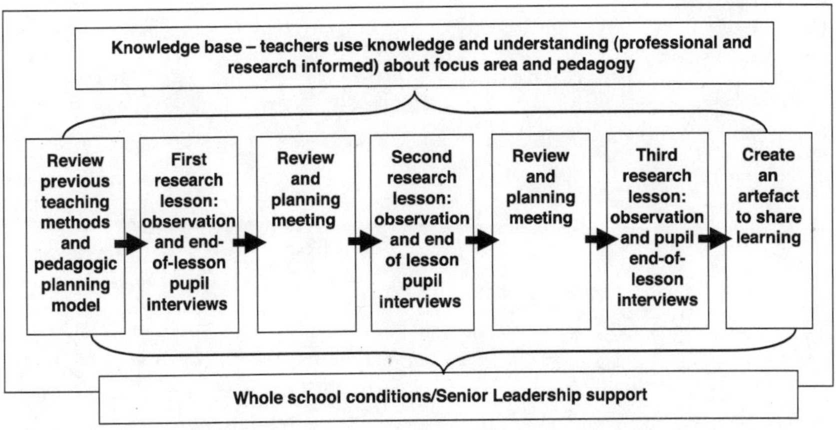

Figure 2.2 *Lesson Study cycle in the Lesson Study-MLD research project*

Case pupils and pupil involvement in Lesson Study

Ways to improve teaching of children with moderate learning difficulties

Two features of the model of Lesson Study were developed through my pilot in the UK (summary findings of which are set out in Panel 1) and these two features were adopted fully into the Lesson Study-MLD project.

The first of these two features is the identification and use of 'case pupils' in the research lesson planning and analysis processes. The second feature is the systematic involvement of pupils in the process of Lesson Study through the elicitation of feedback from pupils on their perspectives of research lessons and of their thoughts for subsequent teaching.

Panel 1. Outcomes of the Lesson Study pilot study in England

The following points emerged from the pilot:

- Lesson Study was found by all teachers involved to be an engaging and replicable process for innovating, transferring and improving teaching and learning practices.
- Both school leaders and teachers in schools involved in the study strongly believed that the Lesson Study process encouraged risk-taking and a culture of professional learning both from what does not work as well as what does.
- Participants valued the fact that a research lesson is jointly owned by participants and felt this increased the likelihood of risk-taking and learning.
- The use of case pupils sharpened teachers' abilities to observe critically important aspects of their pupils' learning that they do not normally get a chance to see.
- The Lesson Study process proved useful for transferring practices across subject areas in ways previously not encountered or envisaged by participants. (A number of lesson studies involved teachers from, for example, the science and music department in a school, the modern

and foreign languages (MFL) department and a science department. Lesson Study may thus have a significant role to play in tackling within-school variation.)

- The process was found to help teachers – experienced and less experienced – to 'see things differently' (project member); to be able to view their own practices critically without being blinded by familiarity or 'blinkered by . . . assumptions about [their] immediate settings' (Desforges, 2004: 6).
- Participant teachers and leaders viewed the process positively as a mechanism which lends itself to cross-school and cross-phase working, particularly as a result of the fact that the unit of study and delivery is a 'lesson'.
- Teachers in their first three years of teaching found that engagement in the process gave them an opportunity to engage in 'deep' professional learning, not offered by existing models such as the standard diet of the induction year. It was used enthusiastically by trainee teachers whose tutors felt it provided valuable structured opportunities to learn from more experienced colleagues while actively engaging with them in joint teaching, observation and analysis.
- The process provided a useful means of addressing common questions and problems encountered by teachers in pedagogic fields of metacognition found within assessment for learning and thinking skills.
- In all cases, teachers found that the value of the Lesson Study was significantly increased when pupils were involved in the process themselves.
- There was evidence of significant positive effects upon pupil progress and outcomes and no evidence of negative effects.

Summarized from Dudley (2007, 2011).

I will now describe these two features in more detail.

Case pupils

Usually, the Lesson Study group identifies between three and six pupils to become the particular foci in research lessons. The choice of which pupils should become case pupils depends on the purpose and focus of the Lesson Study. If your Lesson Study is designed to find out how you can teach history more effectively to a group of boys in your class who seem to find history boring, then it would be most sensible to focus particularly on three of these pupils when you and the rest of the Lesson Study group are planning the research lessons. It would also make sense to observe these pupils particularly closely in the research lessons themselves, and again to discuss their learning and behaviours in detail when you hold your post-lesson discussion. On the other hand, your Lesson Study may not be primarily focused on specific pupil needs or behaviours. It may have a more general improvement purpose, perhaps with a research question such as, 'How can we improve the way we introduce the concept of ratio to year 3 classes?' In a Lesson Study with a focus like this, you are more likely to want case pupils who represent a straightforward *sample* of the learners in the class as a whole, or who may typify groups of learners in the class. Many groups would choose to sample a higher-attaining, a middle-attaining and lower-attaining pupil in mathematics in a Lesson Study with a focus such as this.

Now to answer the question – 'Why have case pupils?' There are several reasons. Case pupils are real pupils who exemplify the challenge presented by different typical learner groups (as in the second example above) or who, for one reason or another, represent learners you have identified as a challenge in the curriculum area of focus (as in the first example above where some found it boring). Because they represent a real challenge, these case pupils hold the Lesson Study group to account for their learning, as I shall explain below.

Let me illustrate what I mean by drawing a comparison. Teachers in the UK have traditionally tended to plan their teaching and to teach alone. In doing so, they might typically consider how they will make sure that their lesson is accessible to differing groups in the class, and perhaps even for one or two outlier individuals operating at levels well below or well above that of the 'average' in the class. This is broadly true even in contexts where primary teachers of the same year group plan a week's teaching together. What can easily happen in contexts such as this is that, despite identifying learning objectives or learning 'intentions' in these plans, the majority of the thinking goes into planning the activities through which the learning intention will be realized. The influence of Ofsted and the National Strategies has also led to a focus in many English classrooms on ensuring that the lesson has certain component parts – a starter, a main activity, a plenary, and so on.

When a typical teacher teaches this typically planned lesson to a typical class of 30 plus pupils, they will be doing so while dealing with the speed and complexity of the classroom, which is one of a most complex work environment. Lewis (1998), Stigler (Willis, 2002) and others have reported on the power that Lesson Study has to slow down the 'swiftly flowing river' of a lesson (Lewis, 1998: 50). My own research into the use of case pupils in Lesson Study (Dudley, 2011, 2012) demonstrates how they can act as powerful brakes in this respect, forcing the attention of observers on the learning of selected, specific pupils repeatedly throughout the research lesson.

However, case pupils also act as catalysts in helping teachers to see evidence of pupils' needs and abilities that they did not previously know existed. This is because when teachers are planning a research lesson, they imagine collectively – and in great detail – how the class will respond to the components of the lesson which they collectively rehearse and build together. They are also forced to *imagine* how each case pupil, with their particular needs and challenges, will respond to these components of the lesson. As they do so, they often modify the components in order to match them more closely to the specific needs of the case pupils and, once satisfied, they collectively record these 'predictions' in the 'case pupil' column of the research lesson planning pro-forma (see Figure 2.1). So, even before the research lesson has been taught, the Lesson Study group has been made to *account* for the imagined learning of the case pupils by being forced to imagine collectively, in great detail, and to record how they think these pupils will respond to the research lesson components and from time to time to act upon these imaginings by modifying the lesson plan (Dudley, 2013).

Lesson Study also holds the group to account for the learning of these pupils a second time. The group's 'imagined' learning represents the sum of the knowledge of the case pupils that is held by the Lesson Study group members. As the group members observe the research lesson being taught, they use the imagined learning notes in the lesson plan as prompts against which to check the *actual* learning behaviours and responses of the case pupils. Now because lessons are such busy, complex and unpredictable occasions, there may be all sorts of reasons why the case pupils did not conform to the expectations set in the predicted behaviours of the research lesson plan. But very often the reasons why the observed responses and behaviours are very different from those predicted by the Lesson Study group's collective imagining is because the Lesson Study group's sum of knowledge about a case pupil is either lacking or simply wrong. For example, the pupil may in fact be operating at a very different level from that predicted by the group from their collective knowledge of the pupil and from the assessment information held in the teacher's records. I have reported elsewhere (Dudley, 2011, 2013) that up to 30 per cent of agreed case pupils' assessments have been shown through the Lesson Study process to be dramatically inaccurate. For all such pupils, this alone is sufficient to change the way they are subsequently taught and to make an equally dramatic difference to their subsequent learning and progress rates as a result.

Lesson Study group members consistently report that the experiences of initially imagining and then systematically observing and interpreting the learning behaviours of case pupils, are revelatory (Lo and Ko, 2002; Dudley, 2005, 2013). 'Focusing down on the case pupils has enabled a number of really important things to be revealed' (Lesson Study pilot teacher, in Dudley, 2012: 89).

They report observing qualities and abilities in the case pupil that they had never known the pupil possessed. Furthermore, they consistently report that having observed a particular trait or characteristic in one of the case pupils, they can immediately see that the trait or characteristic is evident in other pupils in the class (Dudley, 2011).

We can see then that the systematic attention to the learning of the case pupils holds members of the Lesson Study group to account for their imagined learning (in the planning discussions), for their actual learning (or lack of learning) in the observations and post-lesson discussion and of course for their re-imagined learning in the next planned research lesson. We can also see that this accountability extended beyond the learning of the case pupils, because the Lesson Study group members – particularly the teacher whose class was being used for the research lesson – will often see that there are pupils with similar characteristics and needs who will thus also benefit from the intervention or approach that is being developed in the Lesson Study.

The use of case pupils was important in the design of the Lesson Study-MLD project because of the frequent weaknesses in assessments of the needs and functional abilities of children with learning difficulties (see Chapters 1 and 6 for more details about the confusion in identifying MLD). It is clear that a device like Lesson Study case pupils can provide detailed teacher knowledge of student learning needs and so contribute to the assessment and teaching of pupils whose learning needs and support are often misunderstood in schools; pupils with learning difficulties.

The involvement of pupils in providing feedback on learning in the research lessons

Teachers involved in the Lesson Study pilot, and in subsequent research reported elsewhere (Dudley, 2011, 2012), have also reported that the systematic elicitation of feedback from pupils on their experiences of learning in the research lessons is always very informative in adding to their understanding and interpretation of the pupil learning behaviours observed during research lessons. Many have also reported that the contributions of pupils to this process can revelatory and insightful.

Teachers often take a group of students aside immediately after a research lesson and use questions such as those set out in Figure 2.3 in order to gain a sense of the pupils' perspectives of the lesson just taught.

Exactly what any teacher intends students to take away as the key learning points from a lesson and what the students actually take away can differ dramatically – even unrecognizeably – and with alarming frequency (Nuthall and Alton-Lee, 1993). Discussions such as these post-lesson interviews provide teachers with a pupil's eye views on the answers to the kinds of question set out in Figure 2.3 and can thus help to expose and even to bridge gaps in understanding of the pupil learning behaviours observed and analysed after the research lesson. In East Asia, it is also common to have post-research lesson discussions with a group of students, but these tend to be conducted in order to ascertain the degree to which the pupils have attained the learning objectives of the lesson. However, following the development of this more formative approach in the UK, considerable interest has grown in adapting this for use in East Asian contexts.

The gathering of pupil perspectives was important in the Lesson Study-MLD project for similar reasons to those for using 'case pupils'. It is important to gain as much purchase and detail of the perceptions of learners about their learning, and particularly of those learners whose needs are often least well understood. Chapters 4 and 5 describe the impact of the systematic gathering of pupil perspectives, the contribution pupils made to the design of research lessons and the development of some key professional knowledge in schools participating in the Lesson Study-MLD project.

Suggested questions for a post lesson interview with the case pupils	
What did you enjoy most about that lesson? What did you learn? (What can you do now that you could not do? What can you do better? How is it better?) What aspect of the teaching worked best for you? If the same lesson is being taught to another group what would you change? Why would you change that aspect?	

Figure 2.3 *Post-lesson interview questions for case pupils*

Source: NCSL (2005)

Lesson Study: a fruitful teacher-learning model for pupils with learning difficulties

The above section highlighted two aspects of the UK model of Lesson Study that promised to lend themselves to improving teachers' abilities to help children with moderate learning difficulties to learn well. However, this will only happen if teachers' practices change as a result of what they discover and learn about their pupils' learning.

This final section deals with the effectiveness of the Lesson Study model in changing teachers' practices. I will first summarize what we know about teacher learning models that makes a difference to improving classroom practice, and then test Lesson Study against this knowledge base. I then outline some intrinsic features of Lesson Study that promote successful teacher learning about pupil learning, and finally explore why a key feature of the *pupil* learning model in Lesson Study may also be relevant to the role of Lesson Study in helping *teachers* better to support children with moderate learning difficulties to 'attain the objects of their learning' – to succeed!

Teacher learning and Lesson Study

A number of recent, large-scale, studies have examined the features of professional learning that most impact on classroom practice and pupil learning (Cordingley *et al.*, 2004; Pedder, 2006; Opfer and Pedder, 2010; Pedder *et al.*, 2010). They suggest that:

- effective teacher learning takes place over months (not days);
- the classroom is the central location of professional learning activity;
- experimentation or enquiry features in the teacher learning process; and
- there is collaboration with one or more other professional(s) as part of that process (Dudley, 2011).

Guskey (2002) has shown that teachers often have strong beliefs about pedagogical approaches that they have employed over periods of time. He suggests that they are only willing to drop these approaches in favour of new ones if they are repeatedly confronted with evidence from the pupils they teach of the greater efficacy of the new approach. Barber *et al.* (2010) have noted that in the world's most improving and highest-performing school systems teachers take responsibility for professional learning by systematically sharing successful practice and by routinely making practice public. Robinson *et al.* (2009) presents compelling evidence that a powerful single action that a school leader can take in order to enhance student achievement is to engage in collaborative enquiry into improving learning outcomes and teaching in the school. So the components of Lesson Study described above map closely onto the overall model of professional learning described in this section.

I have also reported elsewhere on the promotion of effective teacher learning that is achieved through the following intrinsic features of teacher learning found in Lesson Study. These include features that promote *teacher learning about pupil learning* (Dudley, 2011, 2013):

- Lesson Study group relationships and teacher-talk during teacher learning provide opportunities to explore imagined teaching and to interpret observed teaching in detail and depth;
- creating safe zones to experiment with teaching and learning;
- tapping teachers' tacit knowledge through group planning, rehearsal and group analysis of micro-level teaching episodes;
- confronting evidence from observed pupil learning that challenges *prior* beliefs about pupils as well as about teaching; and
- passing on the newly gained knowledge to others and the importance of this for teacher retention of new teacher knowledge and long-term changes in practice.

A common theme of the above features is collaboration over detailed aspects of planned and observed teaching. From the perspective of activity theory (Wertsch, 1981), the secret to the success of Lesson Study is the way that it holds the members of the Lesson Study group to account for what it wants case pupils to learn; this is the *learning intention* or *learning objective*. Evidence from this school of thought suggests that Lesson Study processes bring the object of learning into sharp focus, and that the Lesson Study group members and their students share a common understanding of the precise nature of the object of learning as a result of the need to achieve this collective understanding (Lo and Marton, 2012; Ko, 2012; Runesson and Gustafsson, 2012). These researchers believe that this shared conception of the object of learning amongst teachers and pupils is strongly promoted by Lesson Study, and can be further enhanced by the use of 'variation' learning theory (Pang and Marton, 2003).

This leads to the final point of this chapter. If Lesson Study improves understanding of the object of learning, then this can be seen to underlie how Lesson Study can be used to improve learning of *pupils with learning difficulties.* This is in the context of how the use of case pupils has already been shown to improve teachers' knowledge of their pupils' abilities, motivations and needs. In order to illustrate this point I will make reference to neo-Vygotskian activity theory triangle. This triangle illustrates relationships between learners, what is being learned and adult or teacher as understood through sociocultural learning theory (see Figure 2.4). In this theory the learner is the 'Subject of Learning' (S) who is strongly motivated to grasp the Object of Learning (O). But S can only be fully motivated and capable of attaining O if they fully understand the nature of O and what success in attaining O will look like.

In this model, a good teacher can assist a learner (S) in attaining their object of learning only if the teacher understands:

- the nature of the learner's object of learning;
- the knowledge that the learner already possesses in relation to this object of learning; and
- the precise gaps in the learner's knowledge that will need to be overcome in the process of learning O.

This gap, between where S is now and where S needs to be to attain O, is termed the learner's 'zone of proximal development' in relation to this learning object.

In this model, a teacher can provide the learner with tools and mediating tasks (a very simple example of which would be 'explanations') designed to help S to make that required proximal development and thus attain the object of learning O.

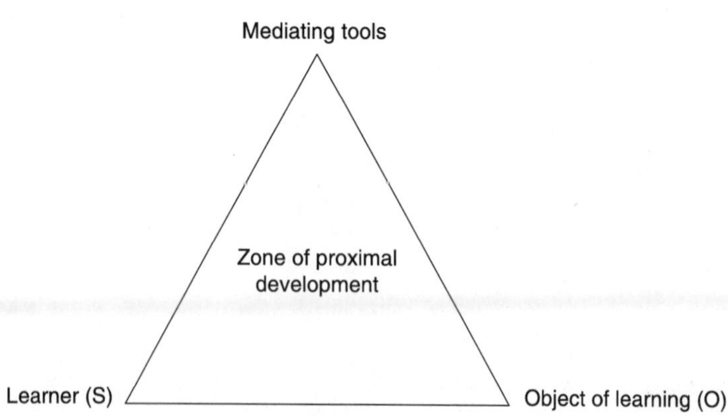

Figure 2.4 *Neo-Vygotskian activity theory triangle*

In conclusion, the model of Lesson Study adopted in this study offers both practical and theoretical reasons to improve teacher learning about how to improve the learning of pupils with moderate learning difficulties. This follows from various assumptions and positions explored in this chapter – (1) that teachers often misconstrue the learning needs of pupils with learning difficulties; (2) that Lesson Study can sharpen teachers' and pupils' understandings of the object of learning in a lesson; and (3) that using case pupils in Lesson Study can sharpen the teacher's understanding of a pupil's precise learning needs.

3

Pedagogy for Pupils in the Moderate Learning Difficulties–Low Attainment Spectrum

Ruth Gwernan-Jones

Introduction

The aims of this chapter are, first, to discuss the category of moderate learning difficulties (MLD), including attempts to define this category clearly, the problems faced in doing so and issues of marginalization and stigma; and second, to review literature exploring special pedagogies developed to support children identified with MLD, and the relationship between special pedagogy and pedagogy in mainstream classrooms. In addressing these aims I will consider the following questions:

- What approaches have been tried in the past and are being used currently to define and identify MLD?
- What does research tell us about approaches to teaching children with MLD?
- Is the category of MLD useful to educational practitioners?
- What skills do mainstream classroom teachers need to teach children with MLD appropriately?

Identification of moderate learning difficulties

In this section, I will discuss the terminology and identification of MLD, survey changes in terminology over time arising from different approaches to definition, and examine the difficulties that have been faced in applying them consistently. This will link current practices and historical practices starting from the time compulsory schooling began. This reflects the ongoing conundrum over whether some pupils need different kinds of teaching, the complexity of making sense of their needs and difficulties for educational practitioners and legislators in structuring provision for their needs. Many of these issues have a long history.

Current prevalence and school census definition

According to the recent DfE (2010/2011) English school census figures about pupils with special educational needs, pupils with MLD comprise nearly one-quarter of all those registered with special educational needs (SEN) at School Action Plus or with statements, making it the most common type of SEN (see Table 3.1).

These figures are based on a definition of MLD provided by the Government to enable reliable reporting in the school census (DfES, 2003). The census collects information about the SEN of pupils at School Action Plus (SAP) as well as those with Statements who have gone through the multi-professional assessment system (see Appendix A in Chapter 6 for more details of these identification stages). Alongside this system, categorization has been and still is used by some professionals (e.g. psychologists) to identify pupils or characterize types of provision (Norwich and Kelly, 2005).

The following definition is given to guide school staff in identifying MLD;

> Pupils with moderate learning difficulties will have attainments significantly below expected levels in most areas of the curriculum, despite appropriate interventions. Their needs will not be able to be met by normal differentiation and the flexibilities of the National Curriculum.
>
> **They should only be recorded as MLD if additional educational provision is being made to help them to access the curriculum.**
>
> Pupils with moderate learning difficulties have much greater difficulty than their peers in acquiring basic literacy and numeracy skills and in understanding concepts. They may also have associated speech and language delay, low self-esteem, low levels of concentration and under-developed social skills (DfES, 2003: 6, emphasis in original).

Below are some points about this definition which draw attention to issues that will be referred to in the discussion below about the complexities of categorizing MLD:

- This definition relies on identification through comparison to peers regarding rate of progress within the National Curriculum, however, there are no attainment cut-off points given for making this judgement;
- Difficulty 'understanding concepts' is reference to low intellectual ability; a within-child reason for the learning difficulty. Possible reasons for the difficulties related to the educational context are excluded ('despite appropriate interventions') and reasons for the difficulties related to larger societal issues such as low socio-economic status (SES) are not mentioned. There are also no cut-off points for what counts as a difficulty in 'understanding concepts';
- Difficulty acquiring basic literacy and numeracy skills is specified; but whether difficulties in other areas, for example science, are relevant is not addressed. This is confusing as children with specific learning difficulties or low attainment often have difficulty with literacy and mathematics;
- Mention of co-occurring difficulties is made; some of which involve some of the other categories of SEN in the census system (e.g. language and communication difficulty; emotional and behavioural difficulty).

The practical process of identifying pupils with MLD can still vary widely. For example, the incidence of MLD as a percentage of numbers of all primary pupils identified with SEN at SAP and with statements ranged from 5.9 per cent in Bournemouth local authority to 49.9 per cent in Knowsley local authority, with the average for all local authorities being 24.9 per cent (DfE, 2011b). Though these figures may reflect differences in pupil functioning between areas, they are also likely to suggest wide differences in interpretation of the category across regions, suggesting governmental attempts at category guidance are not sufficiently clear.

Current terminology

The current system of terminology for SEN in English schools originates in recommendations of the Warnock Report (which were translated into legislation in the Education Act 1981). The Warnock Report was commissioned because changes in legislation brought about by the 1976 Education Act made it a legal requirement that all children, regardless of disability, be educated. Previously education for children with disabilities followed a more medical process. An educational psychologist or doctor assessed children and if they

Table 3.1 Number of pupils by type of SEN reported in the school census in January 2011 expressed as a percentage of all those with SEN. Excludes general hospital schools (DfE, 2011a)

Type of need	School Action Plus		Statement		Total	
	No.	%	No.	%	No.	%
Specific learning difficulty	66,775	13.7	11,360	5.4	78,135	11.1
Moderate learning difficulty	**124,105**	**25.4**	**36,645**	**17.3**	**160,750**	**22.9**
Severe learning difficulty	3,225	0.7	26,045	12.3	29,270	4.2
Profound and multiple learning difficulty	795	0.2	9,100	4.3	9,900	1.4
Behaviour, emotional and social difficulties	127,795	26.1	30,220	14.2	158,015	22.5
Speech, language and communications needs	92,435	18.9	28,175	13.3	120,605	17.2
Hearing impairment	9,480	1.9	6,495	3.1	15,975	2.3
Visual impairment	5,165	1.1	3,610	1.7	8,775	1.3
Multi-sensory impairment	425	0.1	510	0.2	935	0.1
Physical disability	12,905	2.6	14,065	6.6	26,970	3.8
Autistic spectrum disorder	19,470	4.0	42,105	19.8	61,570	8.8
Other difficulty/disability	26,475	5.4	4,000	1.9	30,480	4.3
Total	**489,055**	**100.0**	**212,335**	**100.0**	**701,385**	**100.0**

were diagnosed with a disability, they attended special schools specific to that disability. Treatment in special schools was likely to be more care-focused than educational. At the same time, children in mainstream schools experienced difficulties or obstacles that were overlooked, because they did not fit clearly within categories of disabilities or their difficulties were not sufficiently severe to elicit separate provision.

The Warnock Report recommended a shift away from the use of medical categories that prescribed specific educational placement and/or provision, toward assessing the individual educational needs of a child without reference to categories. The idea was that it did not matter what the difficulty was called, what mattered was what could be done to help the child overcome the difficulty. Previously, stigma associated with categories meant that expectations for children with certain disabilities were very low; for example, children in many special schools did not take exams.

Although The Warnock Report included categories of special educational need, these followed the spirit of their recommendations by replacing medical categories of what was wrong with a child, with educational categories that described areas of need. The previous terminology of 'Educationally Subnormal' (ESN) became 'children with learning difficulties'. Previous subcategories of ESN-severe (ESN-S) and ESN-moderate (ESN-M) now correspond roughly to the current terminology of severe and moderate learning difficulties, SLD and MLD, respectively. The terminology 'specific learning difficulties' (SpLD) was also introduced in the Warnock Report, to distinguish difficulty in a specific area from general difficulty across subjects. Finally, the Warnock Report suggested the use of 'mild learning difficulties', which has not come into common use by practitioners; instead such children might now be referred to as 'low attainers', but the scope of these terms has remained unclear. I will now focus on how these categories are defined and used.

Definition of MLD

Historically, in the English educational system, terminology for learning difficulties has used terms signifying difficulties on a continuum from least to most severe. In Table 3.2, I compare terminology from the 1981 Education Act to the Royal Commission of 1889.

The use of a continuum of terminology where boundaries are not defined except in relation to each other is perhaps a reflection of the purposes for which they were created; 'we have received evidence that there are a great many backward children in our elementary schools who require a different treatment to that of ordinary children' (Royal Commission, 1889, quoted in Copeland 2002: 104).

Table 3.2 History of the development of terminology in England for what are now called 'Children with learning difficulties'

Time period and defining body	Main categorical term	Subcategories on a continuum from least to most severe *Where possible terms representing similar degree of difficulty are grouped by column*			
1981 Education Act	Children with learning difficulties	SpLDs (specific learning difficulties)	MLD (moderate learning difficulties)	SLD (severe learning difficulties)	PMLD (profound and multiple learning difficulties)
1944 Education Act	Educationally handicapped children		ESN-M (educationally subnormal-moderate)	ESN-S (educationally subnormal-severe)	
1929 Wood Committee	Mentally defective children	Retarded children		Ineducable children	
		Dull/backward child	Educable imbeciles or feebleminded		
1913 Chief Medical Officer of the Board of Education	Mentally deficient children	Retarded or dull/backward child	Feebleminded	Imbeciles	Idiots
1889 Royal Commission on the Blind, Deaf and Dumb	Exceptional children	Imbeciles		Idiots	
		Educable imbeciles (feebleminded)	Ineducable imbeciles		

The severity of the difficulty was therefore comparative; teachers teaching large groups of children found that a subgroup of children 'held back' the majority. The subgroup was identified by comparison with the rest of the children in a specific classroom as much as by distinctive individual factors. Variation in the way categories were applied was great; reports of the incidence of dull and backward children ranged from 0.8 to 14.6 per cent in different authorities (Annual Report of the Chief Medical Officer, 1913, cited in Copeland, 2002). Such figures are not dissimilar to more recent educational reports; Ofsted concluded in 2010 that special educational needs were identified in widely varying ways between and within local areas, so that children with similar needs were identified differently according to where they lived and what schools they attended (Ofsted, 2010). Thus, in England there is a long history of definitions of learning difficulties along a continuum of severity, which supports adaptation according to context, but results in variations of identification and provision between settings, for children with similar levels of severity. Many consider it to be unfair that the same child might receive additional provision through a statement in one local authority and not another, but this assumes that it is possible to 'objectively' define categories of learning difficulty.

Defining learning difficulties through comparison with other children is not the only way the difficulties are defined in relation to context. For example, the teaching style of particular teachers or their level of experience may affect how easily some children learn. That learning difficulties like MLD or SpLD or low attainment are not usually identified until a child enters school suggests that it is the context of school that highlights or prioritizes these difficulties. This is supported further because many children identified with disability at school find they are able to cope with the demands of adult life when they leave education. Limited funds also represent a contextual aspect of provision. Following the Warnock Report, a child's local education authority (now local authority – LA) administers statements of special educational needs, a system instigated to ensure legally protected provision for children who experience significant special educational needs. Limited funds require LAs to decide which children should or should not be issued with statements; the result is that decisions about provision in special schools are often dependent on the number of available places. This close relationship between classification of learning difficulties and available places in special schools has been evident since the early 1900s. Burt, a prominent British psychologist up to the middle 1900s, insisted on a lack of clear boundaries between categories of disability on the grounds that 'mental deficiency' was an administrative category rather than a psychological one. He regarded identification as at least partly a practical issue, because it depended on referral from teachers in response to a difficulty in catering for pupils in regular classrooms, and took into account the numbers of available places in special schools (Norwich and Kelly, 2005).

Wider sociological factors also have a role to play in learning difficulties. Children from families with low SES tend to have lower attainment. For example, according to the 2011/12 School Census, 31.5 per cent of primary school pupils with SEN (with and without statements) were known to be eligible for free school meals,[1] compared to 15.2 per cent of pupils with no SEN. In secondary schools, the figures were 26.9 per cent for pupils with SEN and 11.7 per cent for pupils with no SEN (DfE, 2012b).

Legislation can play a prominent role in the way learning difficulties are defined. For example, the Wood Committee (1929) extended the use of 'retarded' to refer to 'educable imbeciles' and 'feeble-minded children'. Copeland (2002) discusses the possibility that the extension was brought about to reduce the number of expensive medical certifications that were needed, as these had formerly been recommended for the feeble-minded as well as 'ineducable' children. That identification practice is linked to issues about the economic cost of provision is currently also relevant. The recommendation of the SEN Green Paper (2011) to reduce the numbers identified at the 'School Action' level of SEN (about half of all identified up to 2013) can also be seen to reflect economic costs and conditions in a time of economic austerity.

These examples suggest that education is a transaction between a child, their teacher, the school environment and wider social and cultural influences. Therefore learning difficulties are a product of all of these rather than only the child. As a result, identification can always vary depending on the context, and the aim of objectively identifying a child's difficulties that ignores social and immediate contextual factors makes no sense. However, a completely contextual view of disabilities is also a problem, as it ignores what the child brings to the interaction that leads to learning difficulties (Norwich and Kelly, 2005).

One approach to coping with the complexity and uncertainty in identifying educational/sociological contributors is to consider disadvantage and educational context separately from SEN. Pursuit of an objective, within-child measure for the identification of MLD is perhaps best represented by the use of intelligence tests. Intelligence tests provide what has often been treated as a measure that gives clear boundaries for identification; however, they also are associated with a number of problems, which I discuss in the next section.

The measurement of intelligence as a means to identify MLD

Interestingly, the uncertainties about identifying learning difficulties gave the impetus for the development of the measurement of intelligence. Binet and Simon (1905), in their original paper describing the assessment of intelligence, referred to the demand for educational and medical assessment of children to judge if they should be educated in special classes or schools. This was the central argument for the need to standardize intellectual assessment (Clarke and Clarke, 1974) on the grounds that it would provide an objective, and therefore fairer, means of assessment. Following the publication of Binet's test, IQ criterion became a common means to identify pupils who needed special provision in many countries. However, Cyril Burt's idea of learning difficulties as a continuum by degree, with scope for consideration of context, has remained prominent in England (Copeland, 2002). At the same time intelligence testing has played some role in assessment since its availability from the early 1900s. For example, during the deliberations of the Wood Committee, IQ boundaries for categories were referred to, and intelligence test results were included in formal medical examination to determine educational placement, until the Education Act 1944. So while intelligence testing has been one aspect of identification of learning difficulties almost from the beginning in the UK, it has commonly been only one aspect alongside others, such as attainment and educational context, unlike other countries (for example the US) where it has been dominant (Detterman *et al.*, 2000).

More recently, the Warnock Report (DES, 1978) reinforced the need for categorization of SEN in practice, while paradoxically also aiming to reduce categorization. The process of allocating additional provision fairly – to the children who need it most – included assessment by professionals that made use of medical categories of disorder and disability. For example, identification for learning difficulties or intellectual disabilities (the contemporary parallel health system term) involves intelligence testing when it follows psychological or health guidelines for categorization, for example the APA DSM-IV-TR, the American Psychiatric Association's *Diagnostic and Statistical Manual of Mental Disorders* (American Psychiatric Association, 2000). Although the classification system requires consideration of adaptive behaviour (for example, impairment in communication, social skills, personal independence, school or work functioning), it also uses IQ score boundary markers to identify severity. For example, it specifies Mild Mental Retardation (MR) at IQ scores of 50–55 to 70; Moderate MR 35–40 to 50–55; Severe MR 20–25 to 35–40; Profound MR below 20–25. Also, the measures of adaptive behaviour tend not to be so well developed or standardized as IQ tests and have been criticized as being subjective. This can mean that the use of category boundaries based on IQ test scores can become the dominant measure (Detterman *et al.*, 2000). In this way intelligence test score boundaries may still play a role in identification of MLD or intellectual disabilities in England, despite lack of guidelines in the education system.

The measurement of intelligence has come under considerable criticism on many counts from the latter half of the 1900s. Figure 3.1 provides a summary of key objections to the use of IQ for assessment of learning

Problems with IQ	Alternative assumptions and approaches
IQ tests provide little useful information to teachers about how to teach children with learning difficulties.	Curriculum-based assessments are an alternative.
IQ tests focus on verbal and logical functioning, ignoring other kinds of capabilities or intelligence.	Adopt broader models of capabilities, e.g. Gardner's Multiple Intelligences; Sternberg's Triarchic theory.
IQ performances are not direct measures of cognitive abilities (they reflect the interaction of cognitive/ motivational and contextual factors.	Use response to teaching or dynamic methods to assess cognitive abilities.
IQ tests do not reliably indicate capabilities to function well in life skills (outside education).	Use adaptive skills to capture a wide range of capabilities in everyday life.
IQ tests involve standard procedures to enable measurement outside real contexts.	Use real context methods such as dynamic assessment.
IQ tests used to identify disabilities and special school placements, when other factors may account for low IQ test performance.	Use ongoing assessment in context to identify special educational needs and provision requirements.
Inappropriate use of IQ test not designed or standardized for some groups, e.g. ethnic minorities.	Ensure the use of culturally appropriate assessment methods.

Figure 3.1 *Problems with the use of IQ scores to identify children with learning difficulties: alternative approaches*

Adapted from Norwich and Kelly (2005).

difficulties, adapted from Norwich and Kelly (2005). These objections centre round the limited kinds of information IQ test scores provide, that they exclude consideration of contextual factors and are relatively inaccurate. The approach of 'objectively' defining MLD through intelligence test scores is therefore widely seen as inadequate. Those categorized with MLD, whether appropriately or not, may experience stigma related to the category, and this is the subject of the next section.

Problems related to identification of SEN and/or labelling

'Labelling' refers to the negative effects that can result from categorizing a child with SEN. It is possible that a person will perceive a child according to their preconceptions of the disability, rather than perceiving the child as an individual person. This is particularly a problem when a disability is associated with high levels of stigma. One of the most highly stigmatized disabilities is that of intellectual disabilities. Once identified the category-based identity tends to be lifelong, and the identity of having an intellectual disability can be treated as primary, with other personal characteristics ignored (Beart *et al.*, 2005). MLD broadly corresponds to criteria for mild intellectual disabilities (AAID 2013). One reason for parent preference for categories like SpLD/dyslexia over MLD for their children is that it establishes that the difficulties are not due to a lack of intelligence (Elliott and Gibbs, 2009). Research in England suggests that children's experience of stigma is not a result of the 'MLD' label so much as peer use of words such as 'thick' (Norwich and Kelly, 2005). However, the category has historical links to the idea of low intelligence, so there is the potential for stigma to result from identifying a child with MLD. Beyond the personal emotional pain linked to experiencing stigma, there is the risk that a child will internalize the notion that they are 'not as good as' others and this can impact self-perceptions and self-efficacy over the life-course (Goffman, 1963).

Interest in the potential impact of teacher expectations related to intelligence was initiated through the work of Rosenthal and Jacobsen (1968). When teachers were given false information about some of their pupils to raise their expectations of the pupils' learning abilities, these pupils' IQ scores did increase. Further analysis attributed pupil improvement to subtle differences in the interactions between teachers and pupils over time. More recent research focused on the relationship between teacher expectations and attainment in natural, rather than experimental, conditions, finds that although the effect is much smaller because teachers' expectations are often accurate, self-fulfilling prophecies can be powerful when a child comes from stigmatized groups (Jusin and Harber, 2005). By extension, the understanding that a child has low intelligence has the potential to influence interactions between a teacher and child in negative ways due to low expectations.

An example of a danger related to the over-identification of SEN was described in a recent Ofsted report (2010). It was concluded that for children at School Action Plus or with a statement, allocation of additional provision was not necessarily appropriate to their needs nor of good quality and therefore did not result in improved educational outcomes. The focus of providers was often on whether additional provision was given or not (for example, in the form of teaching assistant time), rather than the particular learning needs of the child, how well these needs were being met and whether the child was making sufficient progress. The report recommended a shift of focus to the particular learning needs of the child, and the development of approaches that might be taken to meet those.

In addition, the Ofsted report (2010) found that around half of schools used low attainment and lack of progress to indicate special educational needs. The inspectors judged that in fact many of these pupils were actually experiencing poor teaching provision and low expectations. This is an example of how the identification of SEN can focus on the within-child elements of low attainment and 'make invisible' the educational environment. This is a key issue because the government definition of MLD (see above) specifies that the category be based on attainment that is significantly below age norms 'despite appropriate interventions'. A judgement of 'appropriate intervention' is hard to make without greater clarity about the nature of these interventions. This is further complicated because interventions might include both class-level teaching as well as outside-school social and preventive interventions. Working at a class level, there are also difficulties in distinguishing between pupils with low attainment who are identified as having MLD from those with low attainment that might be mainly attributed to socio-economic disadvantage. As Fletcher-Campbell (2004) notes, difficulties in cognition, memory and language, short attention span, inadequate achievement, social skills deficits and emotional problems are common across this range of low attainment. Without more clarity about how outside school social factors adversely affect the intellectual and learning resources that pupils bring to class teaching and learning, it is difficult to begin to distinguish between MLD and low attainment. Also, without further development of appropriate teaching approaches at class level, it will continue to be difficult to identify whether appropriate interventions have been made and so whether MLD is a relevant category. This is where Lesson Study and the project described in this book can make a contribution, as will be shown in subsequent chapters.

Complexity due to co-occurrence of difficulties

Beyond the issues of cut-off points for categorization and the complexity of the interaction of contributing factors to low attainment, categorization of pupils with MLD is complicated by the frequency of co-occurring difficulties. The category of MLD also occurs in conjunction with other SEN (for example language and communication difficulties, motor difficulties, social, emotional and behavioural difficulties and sensory difficulties, as discussed in Chapter 1, see also Table 2.1).

To illustrate the prominence of this issue, a study carried out in a south-west England local authority (Norwich and Kelly, 2005) involved the identification of 100 11–14-year-olds (50 in mainstream and 50 in special settings; equal numbers of boys and girls) who had statements in which MLD was the main significant feature of their identified SEN. Of these children, a large majority (84 per cent) were identified with other SENs in addition to MLD alone (49 per cent with MLD and 1 additional SEN; 33 per cent with MLD and 2 additional SENs; 2 per cent with MLD and 3 additional SENs). The most common co-occurring SEN involved language and communication difficulties (LCD), with 61 per cent of the sample having MLD and LCD identified (and 29 of these 61 children had other additional co-occurring difficulties). Making sense of contributing factors to low attainment becomes more complicated because co-occurring difficulties add additional interactional factors to the low attainment.

Conclusions about the identification of MLD

In summary, there are a number problems associated with the identification of MLD:

1 Complexity and uncertainties:

The definition of MLD both in terms of what aspects of educational attainment are involved and whether intellectual difficulties ('understanding concepts') is involved,

The numerous potential interacting factors that contribute to low attainment (within-child; educational context; societal context; co-occurring difficulties),

A continuum of severity from normal to severe rather than a discrete condition,

Uncertainty about where to draw the cut-off along the continuum; including factors that affect this decision (e.g. the need to provide justifications for low attainment, accessing further teaching resources).

2 Lack of objectivity:

IQ test scores (or other psychometric means to establish within-child factors) provide limited kinds of information and are often interpreted in ways that exclude consideration of contextual factors, so raising doubts about validity,

Although sociological and educational contexts are contributing factors to low attainment, these are not easily measured or identified.

3 In addition, there are a number of risk factors associated with identification:

Stigma

Low expectations

Focusing attention on within-child factors and overlooking educational/social contributors.

Specialist pedagogy for MLD?

These latter issues raise the question of whether to abandon the category of MLD. However, there is an administrative use of categorization in decisions about the allocation of resources and provision planning (Norwich and Lewis, 2005). It is interesting that despite its recommendations to abandon categories, the Warnock Report itself included categories of SEN. This may be because it was recognized that there needs to be a general set of criteria to decide who receives additional resources. However, this does not have to be the traditional medically related one. It might be a set of criteria that also takes into account within-child, social and educational contexts (see Chapter 7 and Norwich, 2013b). As discussed in the introductory chapter, one of the aims of the Lesson Study-MLD project was to examine the MLD category use in project schools. More details about how this was done and what was found are in Chapter 6 and the significance of these findings is discussed in Chapter 7. Further doubt about the usefulness of the MLD category arises from considering whether the category is useful in selecting pedagogic strategies. In the next section, I review the relationship between MLD and specialist pedagogy.

Review of literature about special pedagogy for pupils identified with MLD

Before reviewing the literature it is necessary to clarify what I mean by special pedagogy. I will be following the approach of Norwich and Lewis (2005) in their exploration of special pedagogies across a number of categories of SEN. In understanding what is possible pedagogically they argue there are two positions:

1 **Unique differences position**: in this position, pedagogy is focused on needs that are distinct for individuals and needs that are common to all.

2 **General differences position**: in this position, while pedagogy is focused on needs that are distinct for individuals and common to all

> (just as they are in the unique differences position), in addition pedagogy is also focused on common attributes associated with a group defined by a category. In other words, there are attributes common to MLD pupils and not other pupils that inform pedagogy. This means that how they are taught depends not just on their unique differences but also their *general differences* from others.

The unique differences position recognizes that there are differences in pedagogic strategies but these differ by degree not by kind (as in the general differences position). In their review Lewis and Norwich (2005) use the concept of *continua of pedagogic approaches* to capture the idea that more intensive and explicit teaching tends to be appropriate for children with learning difficulties. Pedagogic strategies range along a continuum, for example, from low *to* high levels of practice to achieve mastery (rather than low *or* high levels of practice to achieve mastery). This notion helps to conceptualize the 'typical' adaptations in class teaching for most children and the greater degree of adaptations required for those with learning difficulties, with placement along the continuum chosen according to the different patterns and degrees of children's difficulties. These are adaptations to common teaching approaches, what have been called specialized adaptations or 'high-density' teaching.

It is important to be clear that the notion of continua of pedagogic approaches does not mean that practical instances of pedagogic strategies at distant points on the continua look the same; they will look different but reflect the same principles. For example, 'high-density' feedback at one end of the continuum would be immediate and explicit, whereas the opposite end might involve self-evaluation. High-density feedback is likely to be more appropriate for children with learning difficulties and self-evaluation more appropriate for high-attaining pupils, but both are strategies to support pupils to evaluate their work.

The point of the continua of pedagogy idea is to reject representing differences of strategy as dichotomies, e.g. high-density feedback *versus* self-evaluation. This notion questions that there is 'typical' differentiation in teaching and separate special teaching or pedagogy; it sees a connection between differences in pedagogy as a matter of degree. As Lewis and Norwich (2005) argue, this position has significant implications for fostering inclusive practice and preparing teachers, because it means mainstream teachers already have a foundation from which to understand and implement adapted pedagogies. This is the thinking underlying why Lesson Study is relevant to teaching pupils with identified MLD, because it provides the space for teachers to extend and intensify general pedagogic strategies, while also providing the framework to evaluate the appropriateness of these choices for specific pupils.

The unique differences position is one often taken by those who prefer a strongly inclusive perspective; those who take the stance of general differences understand that there are pedagogic strategies particularly relevant to groups of children by SEN. This latter perspective is perhaps the most commonly held one; 'there is a persistent sense that special education means special pedagogy to many teachers and researchers' (Norwich and Lewis, 2005: 5). The general differences position can be interpreted as what is meant here by the 'special' in special pedagogy – is there pedagogy that is specific to groups of children identified with MLD rather than those with specific learning difficulties or who are below average in their attainments, but do not have SEN?

In terms of the meaning of 'pedagogy', Norwich and Lewis (2005) characterize teaching as involving three realms, only one of which is pedagogy (see Figure 3.2). Teachers also follow a curriculum, for those in England, the National Curriculum, and the nature and assumptions of the curriculum have an impact on the teaching process. However, in this review the curriculum is not under scrutiny; the question is whether or not pupils with MLD benefit from special teaching approaches in following the same curriculum as their peers. Knowledge is another aspect of teaching, where teachers need knowledge of the curriculum subjects, knowledge about their pupils and knowledge about the way pupils learn. This latter aspect, about the way pupils learn, has relevance to this review, because research suggests there may be knowledge about the way children identified with MLD learn differently to their peers that contributes to the ability to choose appropriate pedagogies. I

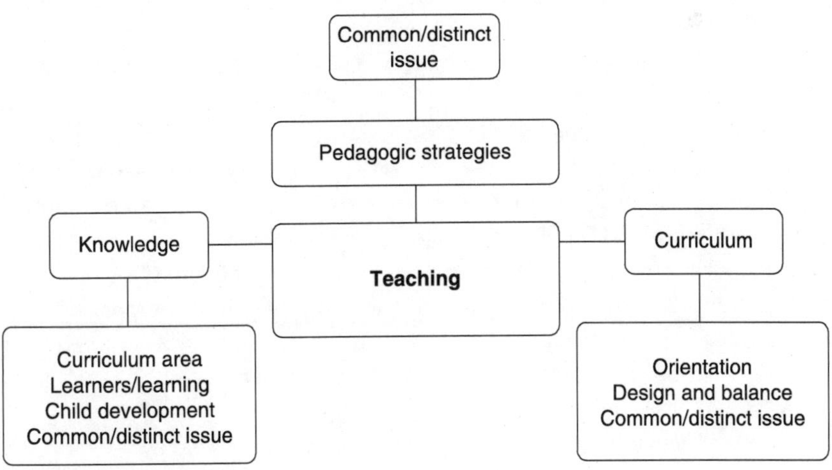

Figure 3.2 *Framework of teaching*

Adapted from Norwich and Lewis (2005).

will examine this topic next focusing on memory and attention. By discussing differences in memory and attention in children with low attainment first, I hope that this will inform the discussion that follows about pedagogy for pupils identified with MLD.

Working memory

There has been some cognitive research that aims to understand what is different about children who score lower on intelligence tests. The two areas that have been most explored are memory and attention (Detterman *et al.*, 2000). Gathercole and Alloway (2008) have recently applied this theory to educational practice. Their simple model of memory and attention consists of three components:

1. Central executive – this is a high-level mental process involved in coordinating storage and effortful processing, e.g. in mental arithmetic. It provides resources that can be allocated to material in any format.
2. Visual spatial short-term memory,
3. Verbal short-term memory.

The verbal and visual spatial short-term memories have limited capacity and work independently of each other.

All components together are known as working memory, and they allow us to hold and manipulate information in our minds for short periods of time. An example of using working memory would be hearing a new word in a foreign language and then repeating it several seconds later. The amount of information that can be held varies; children hold less than adults, and children with low attainment are often able to hold less than their peers. Many people use strategies to hold information in working memory longer, and these may draw upon the two components of working memory – verbal short-term memory (STM), or visual STM. For example, when we rehearse information by repeating it silently to ourselves until we need to reproduce it, we are using verbal STM. When we create a mental image of where in the grocery store an item is located, we are using visual STM. There is also a third component to working memory, the central executive which controls attention. It coordinates what is paid attention to and also has limited capacity.

A very effective means to support working memory is to draw on our long-term memory, by linking the new information to what we already know; one form of this is called 'chunking'. Because working memory has a limited capacity and information remains for only a few seconds, the new information can become lost. So we need to apply strategies to store new information more permanently.

Gathercole and Alloway (2008) screened working memory in several thousand children aged 5/6 and 9/10 and identified approximately 300 children with poor working memory. Of these, approximately 84 per cent had low attainment in reading and/or mathematics. Poor working memory seems to have a close relationship with low attainment; in analysing classroom processes it is possible to identify many explanations for this.

For example, in learning to read a child needs to hold a spoken sound in STM and learn to associate it with a visual letter. As soon as blending and segmenting tasks associated with reading words begins, demands on STM become much greater as the number of sounds and letters increases. To read a child must also hold the words decoded in STM long enough to put them together to create the meaning of the text. Children with poor working memory struggle to meet these demands. In mathematics, learning number operations involves holding and manipulating information. To count, a child has to remember which items have already been counted, while keeping track of which number was last counted and which number comes next. 'Adding on' requires the child to hold the first number in STM while carrying out counting operations with the second number. Poor working memory results in frequent mistakes that give the child fewer experiences of correct answers to make the associations that result in fluent knowledge of number bonds. This prevents the retrieval of already-learned information and requires the child to continue arduous (and often incorrect) calculating procedures (Yeo, 2003).

Difficulties caused by poor working memory are not limited to learning to read and do mathematics. A number of normal classroom procedures put high demands on working memory. Perhaps the greatest is following instructions. Repeatedly over the school day a child is told what needs to be done by whom, where and in what order. This may have to do with organizing a transition within the classroom, sequencing work to be done or communicating crucial information about a task. Children with poor working memory cannot remember all the information, and they often therefore misunderstand what is being asked of them during learning tasks, which prevents them from meeting the learning aims of the lessons.

Another component of poor working memory involves difficulty with attention. Children may begin a task purposefully, but begin to lose focus as they make errors. They become unable to keep in mind the information they need to guide them in subsequent tasks. Research suggests that inattention is often the result of overloaded working memory, rather than inattention being the initial difficulty.

Unlike low intelligence test scores, understanding low attainment as a result of poor working memory provides a framework that offers strategies to support pupils' learning. Gathercole and Alloway (2008) summarize various guidelines for supporting children with poor working memory in the classroom in terms of:

1. recognizing working memory failures (e.g. incomplete recall, failure to follow instruction, place-keeping errors and task abandonment),
2. evaluating working memory loads (e.g. by lengthy sequences, unfamiliar and meaningless content, and demanding mental processing activities),
3. reducing working memory loads when necessary (e.g. reduce amount, increase meaningfulness and familiarity of the material to be recalled, simplify mental processing and restructure complex tasks),
4. repeating important information,
5. encouraging use of memory aids (e.g. wall charts and posters, useful spellings, personalized dictionaries, cubes, counters etc.),
6. developing the child's own strategies to support memory (e.g. asking for help, rehearsal, note-taking, use of long-term memory etc.).

In terms of a general versus unique differences position, supporting working memory as a pedagogic strategy follows a unique differences position, because those who benefit from it are not specific to MLD. In the Gathercole and Alloway study (2005), some of the children with poor working memory did not have low attainment, although they were in the minority. Studies have associated mild intellectual disabilities with poor working memory (e.g. Van der Molen *et al.*, 2007), but presumably, there are also children with low attainment who do not have poor working memory. A number of categories of SEN besides MLD are associated with poor working memory, including SpLDs and ADHD (Jeffries and Everatt, 2004; Kofler *et al.*, 2008). Teaching strategies informed by working memory may be relevant to pupils identified as having MLD or mild intellectual disabilities, but they may also be relevant to other pupils too. Thus these pedagogic strategies are best applied on an individual basis, in accordance with the unique differences position.

Having discussed the role of memory and attention in learning difficulties, I will now turn to special pedagogies for MLD. Fletcher-Campbell (2004), in her review of pedagogy for MLD, begins by discussing the problems in definition of MLD. It is clear that an ill-defined group, with inherent variation between children, is unlikely to have a unique pedagogy that is capable of meeting educational needs because the needs of the group are so varied. She characterizes the literature as 'non-committal rather than confirmatory' (2005: 187). In summarizing pedagogy for these pupils she concludes that:

- they can work alongside mainstream peers on a similar programme of work;
- they do not require any particular technical aids;
- differentiation for this group is based on 'earlier stages of the learning path which their peers have travelled rather than traversing a different path' (2005: 187);
- they do not need an additional curriculum to support MLD-related difficulties (though this may be needed for co-occurring difficulties); and
- specific therapies, interventions or medications are not discussed as being beneficial to this group of pupils generally.

However, she cautions that these comments are as much reflections of current practice with this group as the results of a corpus of pedagogic research. Research seemed to point to matters of ethos, related to the location of intervention and wider learning environment, rather than the content of the intervention itself. She concludes that there was no evidence for a pedagogy specific to MLD; and that a unique differences position, where differentiation is in response to a particular pupil within a background of shared pedagogy, was supported.

Early intervention

In this section, I summarize briefly an intensive early intervention programme that shows a combination of prolonged support outside and inside schools. The intervention was focused on children from families with low SES seen as at risk of intellectual disabilities/MLD, and aimed to improve cognitive and educational levels. The Abecedarian Project (Ramey and Campbell, 1992) was an early intervention programme begun in 1972 in North Carolina in the US with just over 100 children. The intensive intervention programme began in infancy (average nine weeks). Both experimental and control groups received free medical care and nutritional supplements over the course of the programme. The educational element, with which only the experimental group was involved, included intensive levels of high-quality all day and year-long daycare focused on language development. At age four, the experimental group were 10 points higher on a General Cognitive Index (101 versus 91; a statistically significant difference).

The follow-through phase of the study then began, involving educational intervention in addition to regular schooling. This involved half the children from the experimental group receiving the educational intervention and half attending regular school; while half of the control children received the educational intervention and half just attended regular school. Thus, there were four groups:

1. received intervention from birth through early school years,
2. received intervention from birth until school began,
3. received no intervention until starting school, and
4. received no intervention.

Children receiving the additional intervention had a graduate-level home–school liaison officer who supported the child's teacher and parents. This involved reviewing progress and supporting home-based learning activities. Assessment showed that children who received the pre-school and additional education interventions had significantly higher cognitive scores than the other three groups, but the difference was not large. However, the average attainment scores group 1 (full intervention) compared to group 4 (no interventions) were greater (41st versus 19th centile for reading; 51st versus 33rd centile for maths respectively).

A follow-up study of the children who had the full intervention found persistent positive outcomes when they were 21 years old (Campbell *et al.*, 2002). They had significantly higher scores on intellectual and academic measures, attended education for significantly more years, were more likely to continue to higher education and were less likely to have teenage pregnancy compared to the controls. Although children who received the school-age intervention showed benefits, most were not significantly different from those without any intervention.

The Abecaderian Project is unusual in its intensity and length of intervention; it is also unusual in that the intervention involved social as well as educational aspects of low attainment, by providing medical/nutritional and parental support. That this kind of intervention improved attainment levels supports the contention that factors such as low SES make an important contribution to low attainment for these children. However, the interventions involved are not ones that teachers can employ themselves, and cannot be related to the issue of general versus unique differences for pedagogy. It can be related, though, to knowledge that can help teachers understand the way children learn and might influence pedagogy indirectly, for example through awareness of the importance of the teacher–parent relationship in supporting pupils.

Teaching general intellectual and learning strategies: instrumental enrichment

Instrumental Enrichment (IE), a programme designed for implementation following identification of mild mental retardation (MMR) (now termed mild intellectual disabilities) aims to increase cognitive ability and behavioural strategies (Feuerstein *et al.*, 1988). It follows three stages; evaluation of the child through the Learning Potential Assessment Device (LPAD), modification of cognitive structures and shaping and modifying environments.

The learning potential assessment device is a dynamic, rather than static, approach to assessment. Static approaches, as used in conventional intelligence tests, focus on a child's answers to questions unassisted; dynamic assessment focuses on how the child responds to assistance and uses information about what supports learning and about learning gains as the focus of assessment. Mediated learning refers to what the child gains from teacher support. Thinking in these terms allows the teacher to understand why the child is unable to answer questions and then to plan the intervention.

At the second stage, IE is carried out to modify cognitive structures. Rather than teaching content, the focus is on teaching cognitive strategies of how to think and learn. There are three foci for this approach that cover input, elaboration and output processes. For example, in a counting exercise the child would be taught left-to-right, top-to-bottom principles. These principles about effective information-gathering are mediated in slightly different situations until the child is able to apply the strategies independently. In elaboration, the child is taught to integrate the information they have gathered with what they already know, or what they may need it for in future. In output, the child is taught to formulate an answer based on the information they have gathered, and how it relates to what they already know and/or the format of the request. They are taught to take their time to think through what they need to do before responding. In the final stage changes are made to the wider environment to make it stimulating for the child. Appropriate challenge needs to continue for them to apply and develop their learning further.

There has been much evaluative research about the effects of IE. Despite some criticisms of the initial studies (Determann *et al.*, 2000), more recent studies indicate positive outcome effects. Ben-Hur (2000) in his review suggests effect sizes of 0.7 standard deviations for gains in non-verbal reasoning and significant gains in academic achievement. More recent international studies suggest lower effect sizes (0.3–0.5) but also effects on academic levels, self-concept and motivation (Kozulin *et al.*, 2010).

It might be thought that IE represents a special pedagogy for MLD, because it was designed specifically for children with difficulties related to MLD. It may be that its success is due to the use of mediated learning, which prevents working memory overload sufficiently for pupils to be able to reason and/or store information in long term memory more effectively (Bruttin, 2011). However, like the working memory interventions discussed above, these approaches have been shown to be useful for other children with SEN and for those not so identified (Kozulin *et al.*, 2010).

Conclusions

In light of the pedagogical strategies reviewed here, it seems that approaches that are effective in supporting pupils with MLD align with a unique differences rather than a general differences position. The focus is on particular pupils' characteristics and the intensification of general pedagogic strategies relevant to these needs. Where pedagogical strategies focus on general cognitive processes and strategies (working memory or cognitive modifiability) these are not specific to MLD. They relate to pupils with other difficulties and disabilities too as well as those without SEN. These ideas about continua of pedagogic strategies and intensification of general strategies have some similarities with other current ideas about inclusive pedagogy. Florian (2010) describes inclusive pedagogy as extending what is ordinarily available in the community of the classroom. Her argument is that teachers do have the skills to teach pupils identified as having SEN, and by implication with MLD. This is an approach that focuses on the way pedagogic strategies are used rather than matching an intervention type to a specific category (Rix *et al.*, 2009; Davis and Florian, 2004; Cook and Schirmer, 2003).

This chapter has examined the underlying issues concerned with pedagogy for pupils identified as having MLD. This started with a consideration of how categories have been defined and used in relation to those who have come to be identified as having MLD. The problems over defining this category and its relationship to informing teaching have also been explored. This sets the backdrop to the book and the Lesson Study approach to developing teaching for these pupils. I have argued that categories required for administrative purposes are not necessarily relevant to pedagogic decisions. Through a continuum of pedagogic strategies, classroom teachers can develop their teaching to support more pupils effectively. This is where Lesson Study provides a very promising strategy to intensify teaching strategies to better provide for those who struggle with their learning.

Note

1 Free school meals are considered to be an indicator of socio-economic disadvantage.

PART TWO

Lesson Study in Practice: Case Studies

Part 2 is made up of two chapters (Chapters 4 and 5) designed to describe and analyse the work of practising teachers who have used Lesson Study approaches in different curriculum areas and in differing phases in schools. The examples of Lesson Study will focus on where the case pupils had learning difficulties or were struggling with learning, mainly from the Exeter University Lesson Study-MLD project. Compiled by Di Hatchett and Gill Jordan, the chapters cover key aspects of the specific work done through the various stages of Lesson Study through to the outcomes for the pupils, lesson preparation and teaching, professional development and wider lessons for school development. These case studies are intended to contribute rich descriptions of the Lesson Study process and outcomes and to illustrate how Lesson Study is done in practical terms; what developments in pedagogy arise from Lesson Study; what professional learning takes place; and what schools derive from Lesson Study. The names and details of the schools and teachers in these Chapter 4 and 5 case studies have been changed to ensure anonymity.

4

Teachers' Lesson Study Practice in Primary Schools

Gill Jordan

Introduction

In this chapter, I will describe and analyse the work of practising teachers who have participated in Lesson Study projects in three different areas of the UK. The case pupils selected by the teachers, and included here, all had learning difficulties or were struggling with learning. The cases are informed by the case reports written by individual teachers who reported on their lesson studies. These case reports were summaries of what had been done during the Lesson Studies and the outcomes of the Lesson Study cycles. As consultant to these Lesson Study teams, I have drawn on these case reports and supplemented them with background information about the schools and the Lesson Study preparations to produce these illustrative case studies for this book. These case studies are presented as insider accounts of Lesson Studies, in contrast to an external evaluative perspective on Lesson Studies presented in Chapter 6. The details about the lesson studies, the school and local authorities have been made anonymous.

Case study 1: West Park School (as part of the Acorn Network Lesson Study project)

Context and aims

As part of a school-led action research project, groups of primary schools across Southshire identified priority areas for development. The Acorn

Network identified 'writing' as their key priority for the year 2011/2012. With support from Southshire's Learning and Improvement Service, it was decided to use a Lesson Study approach as a means of collaborative planning, teaching, observing and reflecting on learning, in order to maximize pupil progress.

The project involved 33 teachers from 18 Acorn Primary schools, starting in early 2012 and concluding in mid 2012. It was designed to provide professional development for teachers on effective strategies for teaching writing and to ensure that all involved had a good knowledge of Lesson Study – its principles, process and protocols. This Lesson Study project differed from many others in that teachers worked with colleagues from other schools from the outset. It is more usual for Lesson Study to be embedded within a school system before cross-school work commences. The schools' head teachers had made the decision to work in this way.

Preparation for and design of lesson studies

The professional development course designed to support this project was spread over four days. The first training day (Training Day 1) was dedicated to introducing effective strategies for teaching writing and was attended by two teachers from each of the participating schools. Training Day 2, which took place the following day, was attended by the teachers, together with their head teachers, and focused on Lesson Study – its origins, global spread, developments in the UK and the principles, processes and protocols. Two further days were planned for teachers to provide feedback and to disseminate their findings.

The expectation was that teachers would work across three, or in some cases, four schools and would complete their first Lesson Study cycle (i.e. three research lessons) before the third training day in April. The second and third cycles would follow in May and June 2012.

In order to evaluate the success of the project, all teachers identified two case pupils who they assessed at the beginning and at the end of the project using Assessing Pupils' Progress (APP) – a structured approach to assessment that equips teachers to recognize and make consistent judgements about their pupils' learning in reading, writing and mathematics. In line with a school's assessment policy and practice, teachers periodically reviewed evidence of pupils' learning, using the APP assessment guidelines to build a profile of their achievements. APP helps teachers fine-tune their understanding of learners' needs and tailor planning and teaching. Using these assessments, teachers can:

- use diagnostic information about pupils' strengths and weaknesses to improve teaching, learning and pupils' progress;
- make reliable judgements related to national standards, drawing on a range of evidence; and
- track pupils' progress.

The importance of pupil voice was stressed throughout this project. After each research lesson, pupils were interviewed and their responses recorded. Teachers found this to be helpful and fed the information into the post-lesson discussion. As a result, future objectives for these pupils were often adjusted and planning altered according to their needs.

Training Day 3 took place four weeks later (April 2012). This provided an opportunity for teachers to give feedback after Lesson Study Cycle 1. This interim feedback was very positive. All groups had completed their first cycle and all considered they had learnt from the experience.

Table 4.1 Case 1 timetable and design of lesson studies

Timeline	Role of teacher 1 (School A)	Role of teacher 2 (School B)	Role of teacher 3 (School C)
March 2012	Teach 3 research lessons with focus on 2 case pupils throughout	Support planning process, observation, review	Support planning process, observation, review
April/May 2012	Support planning process, observation, review	Teach 3 research lessons with focus on 2 case pupils throughout	Support planning process, observation, review
June/July 2012	Support planning process, observation, review	Support planning process, observation, review	Teach 3 research lessons with focus on 2 case pupils throughout
April–July 2012 When a cycle is completed	Write up case study Prepare Powerpoint presentation (include video where possible)	Write up case study Prepare Powerpoint presentation (include video where possible)	Write up case study Prepare Powerpoint presentation (include video where possible)

School leadership

At the start of this project, all head teachers were consulted and agreed that their schools would take part. They also all agreed on the focus and accepted the terms of commitment laid down by the local authority, which provided funding for the training element.

However, differences in approach, in enthusiasm and in levels of commitment were noted. Most success was evident when head teachers and other members of the School Leadership Team (SLT) had given the project priority and visibility within the school. They provided the required time and support for the teachers to enable them to carry out the Lesson Study cycles in their own schools and in those of their partner schools. In addition, they had encouraged innovation and had taken a keen interest in the new strategies their teachers had adopted as a result of observing practice in other schools.

In the most successful schools, teachers involved in the project shared their experiences with the whole staff, became strong advocates for Lesson Study, and were able to demonstrate the impact on their own learning and on pupil progress. School leaders in these schools were planning how Lesson Study could be sustained and developed further.

Sustaining Lesson Study

During the final event (Training Day 4), there was a discussion around the issue of sustainability – how could Lesson Study develop further within this group of schools? The following ideas were discussed:

- Including Lesson Study as a principle element of the schools' professional development policy;
- Providing dedicated professional learning time for teachers aligned to PPA time (planning, preparation and assessment);
- Linking Lesson Study to performance management, though it was accepted that it should form a part of the process and should not be included in the monitoring of performance by head teachers; and
- Providing those teachers who had taken part in the project with time to present their findings to the rest of the staff and to act as advocates for Lesson Study.

Having seen the success of working across schools, head teachers and senior managers were keen to continue with these arrangements, but many thought the next priority was to identify a core group of teachers in their schools who would further develop Lesson Study. There was discussion about the likely priority for schools and the possible future focus for Lesson Study: specific areas of mathematics. It was agreed that Lesson Study could present good value for money if it created opportunities for teachers to improve their practice and move from being good teachers to becoming outstanding teachers with improved outcomes for pupils.

Lesson Study: West Park Primary School

Context and overall aims

West Park Primary has approximately 210 pupils on roll. It is situated within a suburban housing estate and serves a mixed catchment area of privately and council-owned properties in an area of the town classed as deprived. It had a higher than average take up of free school meals and 22 per cent of children were on the SEN register. The school provides a nurture group, a breakfast club and various after-school activities to enhance the learning of many children. Often, children enter nursery with poor language and social skills.

The focus for this Lesson Study was to improve story-writing in Year 2 using a 'talk for writing' approach. The class had just begun a unit of work on Traditional Tales and the story of Finn McCool was chosen, as it was thought that the characters of the two giants would capture boys' interests. Given that the children's writing of stories was lacklustre, it was considered important that the children learned how storytellers make their tales come to life and engage with their listeners. In addition, introducing new vocabulary to the children was seen as essential to enable them to incorporate it into their writing.

Two boys were chosen as case studies (Case pupil A and Case pupil B). Both were making little noticeable progress in writing.

Research lesson 1

Lesson objective: to use descriptive language to describe the features of a new character.

In this first research lesson, the observers set out to see how the children usually operate within a lesson. Child B had support from a teaching assistant, while Child A worked independently.

The class spent the week getting to know the story. Most had internalized the first part of the story and taken part in several drama activities. They had met a new happy-go-lucky, sporty, but lonely giant. With a group of children they were to decide how he looks and to choose a name and then draw him

Table 4.2 Relevant starting levels and aims for Child A and B

Child A	Child B
Very talkative (leads him into trouble)	Poorly developed speech; speech is unclear and immature
Fluent 'ex-reading recovery' reader (NC level 2A)	Keen and valued contributor to class discussions
Writing at level 1A	Writing level dips into 1C occasionally
Popular	Making fair progress in phonics lessons, but doesn't apply skills to his writing independently
Football-mad	Creative
Assertive	Eager to please
Poorly presented work that is brief, unfinished or missing the point	Hard-working
No sense of pride in his writing	Resorts to copying any text around him if left to his own devices
Aim for child A	**Aim for child B**
To improve his response to learning objectives, time constraints and to ensure a greater sense of achievement and pride in his work	To enable him to apply his phonic skills independently and to write whole sentences relevant to the subject that are a better indicator of his knowledge and creativity

large scale. Finally, still working as a group, they were to add descriptive phrases on Post-it notes to their poster. After a class brainstorming session on how the descriptions could be improved, they used the class' top tips to improve the descriptive phrases which would then be displayed with the giant.

It emerged that child A was aware of the lesson objective and thought he had wasted time in the lesson. He was aware of his writing targets but had not achieved them that day.

The post-lesson discussion revealed observations for each child and led planning for research lesson 2.

Research lesson 2

Lesson objective: to improve writing with time connectives, adventurous language and dialogue.

Table 4.3 Research lesson 1 observations and aims for research lesson 2

Observations of Child A	Observations of Child B
Found it hard to work co-operatively with his peers	Visually stimulated
Talked a lot, but to nobody in particular and his ideas were not adopted by the group	Fully engaged with his group
Worked alone most of the time	Offered original ideas to his group about the giant's features
Wrote his Post-it without consultation with the others	When the writing began on whiteboards his confidence waned
His idea was brief and unadventurous	Appeared unsure of sounds
Helped others to improve on their choice of adjectives when prompted by the teacher	Reluctant to take risks
Took part in the class discussion and appeared to take on some of their ideas. 'He has big stripy feet' became 'He wears stripy football socks with a hole in them.'	Frequently looked at others' boards
Extra time was given to complete the task	Had difficulties sequencing his ideas and forming a sentence
Presentation remained poor	Found it hard to remember his ideas so he could write them down
	Constantly rubbed out and rewrote his sentence
Action for research lesson 2	
The class would hear several reminders of the Lesson Objective and success criteria and a timer would be used to help him work with more urgency.	Child B would be encouraged to refer to a phonic mat and a word bank of key words, labelled pictures of characters, setting etc. He will be trained to use a talking tin to record his ideas.

The focus this week had been on making improvements to sentences. The children invented a new story using their new character. Modelled writing was used to demonstrate and share thought processes and the children used response partners when composing new sentences. This lesson was planned

Table 4.4 Research lesson 2 observations for Child A

Observations of Child A
Did not engage well in discussions about a potential ending
When asked to share ideas he was able to invent an idea on the spot
Offered a low-level 'top tip' for improvement voluntarily
Wrote only one sentence during independent writing
Read his sentence to his partner, but did not improve it
Very distracted throughout the writing session. Time allocated to polishing his sentence was used to continue writing as so much of his time was spent off-task

to enable children to talk about their ideas for good story endings. The success criteria were displayed on the working wall and reference made to them during the lesson. Children were encouraged to stop periodically and read their writing to a partner and to make improvements to it. A stopwatch provided a countdown of time left to complete the task at each stage and would be used to focus children on the task. The guided group used a voice recorder.

Child A

His final piece of writing showed improved handwriting and use of time connectives, but not adventurous language. He was aware of the lesson objective and knew he had not achieved it, but nevertheless he was pleased with his writing. He thought it could be better if the teacher helped him. This prompted the question: what was holding him back? Was it:

- choice of partner
- child's own low expectations
- lack of motivation
- distractions (this includes the stopwatch used)?

Based on this analysis it was decided to use these methods for research lesson 3. So, child A will work with selected partners who will help him focus; the stopwatch will be replaced by a sand-timer, any achievements he has made within the classroom will be acknowledged publicly, guided work will focus on editing, playtimes would be used to pay back time wasted in lessons (as a mad-keen footballer this had a huge impact).

Table 4.5 Observations of Child C in research lesson 2

Observations of Child C
Lacked ideas for writing
Liked using the voice recorders
Recording of sentences appeared to help him spot mistakes in his work
Edited his work using finger spaces and improving handwriting
Copying from his board to his book led to mistakes

Child B and C

Unfortunately, Child B was absent for this lesson and so another child, Child C, of similar ability was observed.

Child C was extremely pleased with his work. The group with the teacher's support used the voice recorders were very successfully, though children needed some training on how to use them independently.

Research lesson 3

Lesson objective: to think twice about word choices and to use all of their senses to write a riddle.

This lesson was planned as part of the 'springtime' topic. The children had undertaken a variety of writing tasks during the week using descriptive language, but had not worked with riddles before. The first part of the lesson aimed to familiarize them with the genre and they read and solved riddles together. They were then asked to write a riddle using familiar spring images as a stimulus. Child A worked independently in his usual place for literacy, a sand-timer was used, frequent reminders about the lesson objective and opportunities to share work with a partner as it progresses were also part of the lesson. The teacher provided feedback on good choices of words and phrases.

Child B worked with the teaching assistant to form simple sentences and improve them before writing them down to make a group riddle. He used a voice recorder and phonics mat.

The Lesson Study team's response to the question, what held Child A back in research lesson 3?, was the incessant talking and the distraction of the timer. He enjoyed getting recognition for his achievements in class, as well as on the football field, and was beginning to take more pride in his work. Child

Table 4.6 Observations of Child A and B in research lesson 3

Observations of Child A	Observations of Child B
Read some of the riddles aloud, but did not attempt to solve them	Really engaged in the picture riddles
Appeared distracted by the timer on the table	Good ideas for the riddle about a frog. 'His legs are squashy'
When everyone else ignored him he finally settled to solve a riddle and wrote an answer on the back	Found it hard to distinguish his words on the talking tins
Appeared inattentive on the carpet, but was clear about the task and lesson objective when asked	Wrote his words and counted them then listened and counted the words
Found it hard to select and settle with one picture	Listened to the sentence over and over again and practised saying it several times
Talked to whoever would listen. At one point he told others to be quiet as he was writing, but then joined in the conversation	Wrote the sentence correctly in his final riddle
Finished basic task, but not the extension	

A seemed to talk through habit, not through necessity and it was hard to find a partner to help him with this issue, so an isolated spot away from distractions was found to work well for him: he often chose to do this. The teacher decided that in future the timer would continue to be used at a distance and a carefully selected response partner would help him to focus on the learning objective.

The Lesson Study team's response to the question of what held Child B back in research lesson 3 was that, although the voice recorder helped, he needed to learn to use it independently. He also found it hard to spot mistakes when writing a whole sentence. Through guided work he was helped to write separate words on cards before inserting them in his writing. A talking partner, it was decided, would help him rehearse sentences before recording them. He will continue to be encouraged to use phonics picture mats when he is stuck.

Impact of Lesson Study

The following quotes from participating teachers capture their evaluation of the effects of the Lesson Study:

On pupils' learning and progress:

Through this project I have been reminded that learning behaviours are developed over time and that whilst some children adopt them readily others need constant reinforcement. Behaviour, as seen in Child A, which counteracts learning can be changed over time, but it is a long-haul task and could not be corrected within three short weeks. Child A and others like him in my class have benefitted from clearer expectations (time constraints, success criteria, etc.) and explanations of what we are learning and why we are learning it. Presenting their work to a partner, the class or their group and not just their teacher has raised their awareness of audience and with that they raised the standard of work.

From the observations I was made aware of the needs of children who find language difficult. Planning will allow time for them to organize their thoughts and give extra rehearsal time to help them achieve. Pictures and actions will be used to help them to remember. Simple procedures to follow when writing are being taught so that they will be automatically adopted, enabling this group of children to function independently in the class room. Pupils like Child B who in addition to under-developed speech have a poor memory will be given aides to support them as they work on their own, encouraging them to work without the support of an adult.

On teaching practices and future teaching:

I have listened to my colleagues' observations and advice and have been able to put into place measures that will help groups of children learn. However, much of my learning has come from observing children in other settings. An engaging lesson that we assumed would be enjoyed by all revealed a shy child who made no progress in the drama lesson taught in preparation for writing. Given a piece of paper to plan his story cartoon-style, adding speech bubbles and extra details he blossomed. Variety will play an important part of my teaching.

The second child I observed helped me to understand that the level of support given to a child can help or hinder significantly. Over reliance on help from an adult prevented learning. The adult did not expect the child to speak in sentences so he did not. She was quick to come to his rescue as soon as he began to struggle so he learned an easy way to get the job done which required no effort. My lowest achievers will be taught how to use resources to become independent learners as far as possible and the expectations for the finished job will be in line with this.

Overall this project has made me consider the variety of ways in which we learn and how to make children take responsibility for their own learning.

> Changes have been made to incorporate not only what we are learning today, but how we are going to learn it; what will I do to help them and what they have to do for themselves.

On school approaches to teaching, learning and to CPD:

> I believe that Lesson Study can have a positive impact on teaching and learning if the school is committed to the time and organization of it. In a small school I think working in trios may be unworkable, but can see that paired study partners may be more appropriate. I think it could work well across year groups if a specific focus is identified and that working collaboratively to address any issues the school/Key Stage (KS) may have in this practical way will have a longer-lasting effect than meetings of individuals working in isolation. The school will be developing ways to teach learning behaviours to children and this might be an appropriate focus for Lesson Study.

Case study 2: Brownleigh School (as part of a Northshire Lesson Study project)

Context and overall aims

This recent Lesson Study project, which was partly funded by the Every Child a Chance Trust, focused on the role of expert teachers in supporting guided group work within their schools. A total of eight primary schools selected a literacy theme and ten schools selected a mathematics theme.

The schools were asked to identify a member of the leadership team to take overall responsibility for the initiative and to ensure completion of all required reporting and dissemination work. In addition, the schools identified two class teachers to undertake the Lesson Study cycles and either the Every Child a Reader (ECaR) or the Every Child Counts (ECC) teacher. These expert teachers have high levels of training and skills in literacy and mathematics and would become part of the Lesson Study group.

The training programme comprised three days. Day 1, for head teachers and teachers involved in the project, was designed to provide an understanding of the Lesson Study process, along with an overview of guided group work and the role of the expert teacher. Day 2 provided an opportunity for teachers to discuss their Lesson Study experiences and practices and Day 3 would be a dissemination event, with head teachers or senior leaders from other interested schools invited. Liaison with the local authorities was considered to be an important element of this project, with advisers identified to monitor its effectiveness, attend training and organize for the dissemination event.

Lesson Study: Brownleigh School

School context and overall aims

Brownleigh Primary school is an inner-city school of 230 pupils, the majority of whom come from the most deprived 1 per cent of wards nationally. At least 80 per cent of children enter Foundation Stage 1 significantly below national expectations, many with speech, language and communication difficulties. Given this profile, it was essential that children make accelerated progress and the school focus on early intervention to raise standards. By the end of KS1, the attainment gap had closed significantly and by the end of KS2, pupils attained above national standards in English and maths. Pupil progress was carefully monitored and appropriately trained staff work flexibly throughout the school where need was identified.

The Lesson Study group comprised the Reading Recovery (RR) teacher (who is also the deputy head teacher), an experienced Year 1/2 teacher with expertise in SEN, and a Year 1 teacher new to the school; all concerned to improve standards of writing.

Pupil attainment in writing was lower than in reading and mathematics in this school. The complexity of the processes involved in learning to write can be overwhelming for some children. A significant problem area that was identified was a lack of knowledge of key words for writing, making the writing process slow and so children became disengaged from the task. It was considered important to address this issue by improving the fast writing of key words, but on a personalized level and ensuring contextualization of the learning. A Reading Recovery learning technique of repeated writing of contextualized words was introduced to the teachers by the RR teacher.

Case pupils

Teachers identified the case pupils for the Lesson Study. The writing of case Pupil A, a Year 2 pupil identified as having SEN, had been assessed at Level P8 (well below age expectations). His handwriting was poor, his phonological knowledge was limited and he had few key words in his writing vocabulary. He disengaged from writing after a very short time and had a very low level of independent learning. Case Pupil B, a Year 1 pupil, who attained at a higher level, needed to develop more independence in his learning.

Research lesson 1

The lesson was taught by the Year 1/2 teacher to the all-boy group of children, who were asked to compose a sentence, with the teacher intervening by providing pupils with unknown high-frequency words specific to their sentence. The teacher wrote these on the pupil's whiteboard. The pupil was then required to 'quick write' the word on the whiteboard before entering it into the sentence in their book. The expectation was that over time they would build a bank of words specifically for their own needs.

Observations of how Child A and B responded is summarized in Table 4.7.

Table 4.7 Observations of Child A and B in research lesson 1

Child A	Child B
Began with a poor writing posture with his hand behind his back	Began with a poor writing posture; was sitting directly next to the teacher who intervened by writing 'has' and 'are' on his whiteboard
He worked quietly with a degree of independence; was not placed directly next to the teacher	Teacher then asked him to use the 'quick write' method to consolidate the learning
Initially he suggested a sentence, which the teacher up-levelled (to support language development). But was then unable to recall the sentence he wanted to write	Was later able to spell 'has' independently for use in a separate sentence
Subsequent sentence was not at all linked to his initial idea	Was given the word 'destroy' on a whiteboard to copy into his sentence
Then wrote 3 sentences, used finger spaces and showed some phonic awareness	Went on to write 3 sentences but began to lose finger spaces towards the end
He had support from the teacher when writing the word 'through', which was given to him on whiteboard	

Post-research lesson 1 discussion

During the post-research lesson 1 analysis, the following questions were raised:

1. Was Case pupil A unable to recall his original sentence because the sentence was changed by the teacher to up-level the language?
2. Did this cause him to feel that he no longer had ownership over the sentence and as a result was not able to recall it?
3. Does our approach as teachers to continually encourage children to improve their work (e.g. by adding adjectives, connectives, etc.) mean that we lose sight of the original objective and the progress made?
4. Does intervening to up-level work further affect the children's headspace and become too much for them to cope with?
5. Should we essentially 'pick our battles' and value the small steps of progress made?
6. How do the abilities/character of the child affect how they cope with intervention? It is important to consider the personalized learning of all children and to take into consideration how much their character/ability can cope with intervention. Interventions not related to the original learning objective may hinder the small steps of progress made.
7. How much would this affect a child's self-esteem?
8. Is the physical position of the teacher, in relation to the pupil, important?
9. What effect does grouping have on learning?

Planning research lesson 2

From these considerations, it was decided to plan research lesson 2 in the following ways:

1. Mixed ability grouping to be introduced.
2. Teacher will move around the group – not remain static.
3. Teacher will not intervene to correct aspects other than those related to the original learning objective, e.g. handwriting, more complex words, change sentence to up-level.
4. Specific, personalized high-frequency words will continue to be written for the child on whiteboards, focused on words appropriate for that level of learning.

Table 4.8 Observations of Child A and B in research lesson 2

Child A	Child B
Started with better writing posture but soon began to lean on furniture	Wrote 4 questions using question words and question marks
At times he was observed using the Year 1 boy as a role model	Was supported to write the word 'you' using the RR model
He then went on to write four questions, using question words and question marks	He was practising writing the word 'you' (the orientation of letter 'y' was incorrect); he was practising this. Teacher noticed this later and the orientation was corrected later
He was supported to write the words 'do' and 'what' using the RR model	Evidence that he had retained the spelling of 'are' from the last Lesson Study session
Written outcome was much improved though session considered too long	His attention began to wander towards the end of the session, but he later said that he liked working with all boys
Teacher felt it was important to intervene in some key handwriting issues if they were becoming habituated and would be difficult to correct at a later stage	

Research lesson 2

The Year 1/2 teacher taught this lesson to a mixed ability group now comprising four boys, including a Year 2 boy with SEN and one higher-attaining Year 1 boy. The latter boy provided a good role model for other boys without his own learning being compromised as the learning within the group was personalized.

Post-research lesson 2 discussion

These points summarize the analysis following research lesson 2:

- The teachers liked the dynamic of having mixed ability children in the group. The more able pupil provided a support and role model for the other children. The task was appropriate for work with a mixed ability group.

- It was agreed that the RR technique was successful as the children have a certain level of independence in terms of simple phonic knowledge and the ability to 'have a go' at writing independently.
- It was felt that having the whiteboards available for children to 'have a go' at particular spellings also worked well.
- Allowing children to have a go at more difficult spellings and not correcting them also allowed the focus to remain on the main lesson objective.
- It was agreed that it was the right decision to correct Case pupil B on the orientation of the letter 'y', particularly as this was included in one of his quick write words. It was also felt that if necessary it would have been appropriate to address any issues with basic punctuation but not appropriate to alter the child's original sentence.

  They discussed the length of the lesson – both children said it was too long. Could the lesson be chunked to support children in focusing on their task? Could the lesson have been chunked into 2 parts; one part to focus on the initial sentence writing and the second part to focus on language development and raising the level?

Planning research lesson 3

From these considerations it was decided to plan research lesson 3 in the following ways:

- To continue working with the same mixed ability children.
- The teacher will pick up on other points of personalized learning, e.g. finger spaces, capital letters, full stops, but would not intervene to improve content.
- The teacher will continue to move around and be positioned in order to support all children.
- Children will continue to be asked to 'have a go' to write more difficult words on whiteboards. These will not be corrected.
- The teacher will continue to follow the Reading Recovery model for teaching high-frequency words.
- The lesson will be chunked into parts to allow the teacher to support children in keeping on task as well as to allow for the opportunity to specifically change the focus/context of their activity to further

accelerate their learning; e.g. Part 1 – write a sentence, Part 2 – improve the sentence (language development); or Part 1 – write a question, Part 2 – answer the question.

Research lesson 3

This lesson was taught by the Year 1/2 teacher with the learning objective for the class being to write a sentence for the beginning of their story. The children continued to work in the same mixed ability group and the teacher moved around the group and gave personalized high-frequency words. The teacher intervened on other key points where necessary in order to develop key learning. This time the lesson was chunked into two ten-minute long sections.

Post-research lesson 3 discussion

These points summarize the analysis following research lesson 3:

- The children had not needed much high-frequency word intervention as they mainly used the class model for support. Could they have been given the first sentence and asked to write the second independently? However, the objective was to write the initial sentence. Could the model have been taken away?

Table 4.9 Observations of Child A and B in research lesson 3

Child A	Child B
He thought of his initial sentence fairly quickly, using the class example as a model	He was able to orally give his first sentence, but kept losing his train of thought as he was writing it, making lots of crossings out
He was given high-frequency word intervention for 'saw' but kept quick writing until he was told to stop	He did not seek high-frequency word intervention support, but was given intervention to write the letter 'g'
He wrote his initial sentence neatly with full stops and capital letters	He very much relied on adult support for encouragement in order to work independently
But found it difficult to write his improved sentence in the next part of the activity	He was able to add an adjective to his work for the second part of the activity

- Case pupil B needed a behaviour change to engage him without depending on adult support. For example, he was not thinking of his sentence while other children were talking and instead waited until he was asked to take his turn. He needed to work on listening and be specifically told to think of his sentence, while the other children are saying theirs. This meant that the teacher will have to continue to specifically direct him until behaviour begins to change.
- Could the children have been asked at the beginning to point out things around the room that would help them to encourage independence?
- Children found it difficult to try and add their adjectives and so had to re-write them. Is this wasting time? Or is it over-learning?
- Could the focus group have worked independently for the second part of the lesson and could the teacher have gone on to work with another group?
- Have children become accustomed to seeing perfect print and finished work and so struggle to see the value of editing and improving?
- Pupils enjoyed working in mixed ability groups and boys liked writing with other boys. Shorter time for activity was a positive move.

Impact of Lesson Study

The following quotes from participating teachers capture their evaluation of the effects of the Lesson Study:

On teaching and pupil progress:

> Impact on pupil progress has been significant. Case pupil A now has a bank of high-frequency words to draw on when writing. Over the autumn term he has progressed from Level P8 to Level 1B in writing.

On teaching and future practice:

> There has also been a significant impact on practice. The technique for teaching high-frequency words is now being used throughout Year 1 and will be introduced to Foundation Stage and Year 2 next term.
>
> There is a need to carry out a critical examination of groupings and the effect on SEN learners. It would seem to be beneficial to employ a variety of groupings in different contexts; limiting children to specific groups can limit learning because peer support is removed.

> Given the complexities of learning to write, the focus of learning at any one time for beginners should be narrow. Intervening on all levels of writing becomes too confusing for this group of learners. This is key for SEN learners, but good practice for all.

Personal reflections:

> The Lesson Study project has been an extremely valuable experience for all involved. It has allowed the RR teacher to use her expertise to impact on classroom practice and as a result the teaching of writing in KS1 has changed. There has been an impact on all learners, including SEN – progress in the autumn term is greater than that experienced in the same period last year. It has been a very positive experience for staff – non-judgemental and highly supportive.

Chapter author's comment about this Lesson Study: as the person who introduced and supported this Lesson Study I would have found it difficult to offer further constructive advice as what had been seen represented outstanding practice.

Case study 3: Platter Primary School

As a result of the Exeter University Lesson Study-MLD project, there has been considerable interest in Lesson Study, especially within the university's partner schools. This primary partnership school had been involved with the university in a number of ways and was keen to consider Lesson Study as a means of extending their professional development programme. An introductory session was held with all staff, during which the history, process and protocols were outlined. As a result, the head teacher invited expressions of interest from the staff. Two Year 1 teachers, together with the Reading Recovery teacher, were keen to take advantage of this opportunity and further meetings took place, in order to provide them with ongoing support.

School context and overall aims

Platter primary school is a two-form entry school for 4–11-year-olds with about 400 pupils. The school aims to provide a creative and inclusive curriculum that will engage and motivate children. The Lesson Study group had a range of experience and expertise across Key Stages 1 and 2 and included expertise in Reading Recovery techniques. The aim of the Lesson Study was to develop teaching strategies in whole-class sessions that would engage and motivate passive and disengaged learners during whole-class sessions, and also to develop independent tasks that would be engaging and accessible to SEN learners. In addition, it was seen as essential to include lots of talk and role play and to help to enthuse the children to provide a strong purpose for writing.

Case Child A: Child A, a boy with behaviour difficulties, was unable to work independently and to stay on the instructed task (he was identified as having SEN). He was assessed at Level P8 for writing at the beginning of the project.

Aims for Child A: to increase confidence in his ability to write independently and to maintain his focus during an independent task without the support of an adult.

Case Child B: Child B, a boy, was a fluent reader and capable writer, but lacked engagement during whole-class session and often struggled to understand tasks for independent work.

Research lesson 1

The lesson objective was to retell the opening of the traditional tale of Rapunzel. It began by asking the children what they already knew about the story of Rapunzel, who the characters where and where it was set. After reading the opening of the story to the children, freeze-framing was used to explore how the characters had behaved and how they had felt, e.g. show me the face you would be making if you were as hungry as the characters were in this part of the story, climb the wall and freeze at the point when you get caught by the witch. Children were brought out of the freeze-frame and questioned in role. The next part of the story was then read: this involved a dialogue where a witch threatens the man with an undisclosed punishment. Using paired talk, children discussed what the punishment might be, re-enacted the dialogue and then fed this back to the class.

Post-research lesson 1 evaluation

Overall the team considered that the lesson went well, with the case pupils showing a good level of engagement throughout the whole-class session. Physical movement worked well. Instructions were clear and children fully understood the task and were engaged during group work. The plenary showed that all children had carried out the drama task with understanding. This provided a good lead into starting the writing in the next lesson; the children were fully immersed in the story and were motivated to continue with it.

Table 4.10 Observations of Child A and B in research lesson 1

Child A	Child B
Initially disengaged but re-engaged when lolly sticks used to encourage talk	He appeared to listen attentively during the whole class session, but sat up and looked more alert when lolly sticks used, again as a means to encourage children to engage in talk
He was reluctant to take part in the drama activity, seemed self-conscious, but keen to do paired talk appropriately	He looked around a lot to see what others were doing during freeze frame activity
During the group task he wanted to change the story so he was the witch. He refused to take part until able to swap and the teacher had to intervene	During the group activity he was dominant but encouraging and actually made sure the group stuck to task; was then keen to show his work at the end
He did then carry out the task well and although shy he did perform to the class. He didn't seem to enjoy the attention from peers	He enjoyed the praise from peers. The knowledge that he might have to show work kept him motivated to do it well

Research lesson 2

This lesson objective was to add detail to part of a story when re-telling it. Children were asked to close their eyes while listening and imagine the picture in their heads. The teacher read the first page of the new, more detailed version of the story. The children then questioned what they had heard in terms of these questions:

- How is this story different from yesterday's?
- What else do we know now that we didn't know before?
- How does the man feel about the lady?
- Do they have a happy life?
- What can they see from their window?
- How does the view make them feel?
- What do they look like?

The children were then asked to write descriptions to add to posters with the following headings on them: The View, The Cottage, The Man and The Woman.

Table 4.11 Observations of Child A and B in research lesson 2

Child A	Child B
He was very keen to answer the questions and provided appropriate responses	He was passive to begin with, checking other children's behaviour
He closed his eyes/hid his face when asked to take part in a simple role-play activity	He was engaged during talk with partners and gave appropriate and considered responses, but became disengaged again after the talk partner session
He was reluctant to talk with his talk partner but keen to talk to the teacher	He did not take part in role play having lost interest in it
Though at times he appeared to be distracted, his responses did show that he was listening	During the activity, initially he tried to get a partner to work with him, took time to start task, tried to distract others and claimed to forget the task
During the activity he seemed keen to start but did not get going until speaking to the teacher; initially he wanted to do the task under his own terms, 'I want to do Cinderella' 'I want to do the witch.'	But he responded well to competitive elements once other children got going and wanted to keep up
He began by copying another child's idea and then did a better one by himself and continued to write ideas enthusiastically. He was very excited to display his ideas	But he showed a consistent lack of self-discipline and motivation except during the competitive element of the lesson
During the plenary he was very engaged, he wanted to contribute and was desperate to be listened to	

The teacher then demonstrated by writing one Post-it for each heading and asked the children to come and put their Post-it notes under the right heading. Children then worked independently to write ideas on Post-its and put them under correct headings. During the plenary session, decisions about the placing of the Post-its were discussed and questions posed.

However, he responded well to competitive elements once other children got going and wanted to keep up. He showed a consistent lack of self-discipline and motivation except during the competitive element of the lesson.

Good-quality writing was observed from both case children and the majority of the class. Children responded well to the immediacy and purpose for writing. It was accessible to all at their own level. The case pupils were less engaged during the whole-class teaching session. Perhaps more visual/kinaesthetic resources were needed, and it was suggested that there was too much teacher talk; needing to be reduced in research lesson 3. The paired talk helped those children with few ideas, but some struggled to generate their own ideas without more stimulus. So the plan for the next lesson was to use more visual/kinaesthetic stimuli and more appropriate use of talk partners.

Research lesson 3

The lesson objective was for children to write the opening of a known story. The purpose of the writing was explained: to write the opening of Rapunzel for another class to guess the story. Three different traditional fairy tale openings were read to the children and they were asked to guess which story was being introduced. They were then asked how they knew. The children then took turns to tell their partner the opening of a chosen story without giving away the name. The teacher then modelled an opening sentence and orally rehearsed further sentences to give children starting points. The children were reminded of the purpose and that they would need to be able to read their work to the other classes. They were told to use their phonic knowledge to spell independently.

Activity: children then wrote the opening of the story in books using the story opening 'Once upon a time' and using sentences from yesterdays

Table 4.12 Observations of Child A and B in research lesson 3

Child A	Child B
He focused well and took part in the storytelling activity in the main teaching session once he was paired with an appropriate partner	He was focused and enthusiastic and worked very well with his partner in the whole-class session
In the main activity he still needed the task to be re-explained by the teacher, but then was confident to write alone and remained focused to the end of the session	He was slow to start his writing, looked around at others but got going once reminded by the teacher of the purpose
He read out his work in the plenary and was immensely proud of his work and re-read it well	He produced a much longer piece of writing than previously and showed increased confidence when reading it aloud

Table 4.13 Summary of attainments following Lesson Study cycle

Child A	Child B
Increased levels of confidence in his writing and is much more able and willing to work independently without constant reassurance and encouragement from an adult	Learned the importance of being able to read back his work and thrives on having a true purpose for a piece of writing
Now very keen to show his work to others; he sees himself now as a boy who can write and enjoys using this method to communicate his ideas	Still needs prompting to focus and start, but once he gets going there is no stopping him
Choosing to write in free planning time	

'harvesting'. They were also told before starting that three stories would be selected and read to children in the other class to see if they could guess the story.

Plenary: groups from the other class were invited to come and listen and to try to guess which story the opening was from. Children were asked which parts from the children's writing helped them to identify which story it was.

Post-research lesson 3 analysis

Both case children produced high-quality writing in the third lesson, showing a large increase in their participation, focus and independence. They both responded very positively to the increased emphasis on writing for a purpose and were keen to produce a high-quality piece of writing at the end of lesson 3. Both children made good progress and moved up a sublevel in a term. It was uncertain whether this was a direct effect of the Lesson Study, but it was believed that the techniques used in this sequence of lessons had a really positive effect on these case pupils' experience of writing and these techniques are now being used regularly in the classroom.

Impact of Lesson Study

The following quotes from participating teachers capture their evaluation of the effects of the Lesson Study.

On teaching practice and future teaching:

- To ensure I give children a true purpose for writing in order to engage reluctant writers.
- Vary teaching strategies used throughout each lesson in order to engage all children (e.g. paired talk, drama activities).
- When planning a teaching sequence have a very clear idea of the desired outcome from the onset and to work backwards from this.
- Use very clear and precise language in order that children follow tasks effectively and are able to fully understand what they are expected to do.
- Set clear expectations before a task and ensure children understand what a 'successful' piece of work looks like.

On the school:

> I have given feedback on my Lesson Study experience and this year we will be carrying out the process in teams of three across the whole school, with a focus on numeracy. Our main challenge will be the organization and cost of the process. At the end of the year we will evaluate the effect that it has had on teaching and learning across the school.

Personal reflections:

> I found the Lesson Study process very valuable to my own teaching. It was a real privilege to have time to observe other practitioners and to give and receive feedback on my own and other's teaching in a non-judgemental environment. Planning as a team was a great experience, we certainly were not short of great ideas! I often now find myself referring back to things that came up during the process and seeing the effectiveness of the concepts learned on my own planning and teaching of lessons. I feel that the process has helped to make my teaching more motivating and stimulating and the observation of pupils has given me a greater understanding of the types of learners that you find in a class and the strategies needed to engage their various styles of learning. We found the organization of the process somewhat of a challenge but managed with the help of student teachers and very capable teaching assistants. It certainly worked the best when we taught the three lessons in a sequence on three consecutive days.
>
> Overall I really valued the experience and am looking forward to taking part in the process again later this year.

Concluding comments about three case studies

These three case studies show that some of the fine-grained detail in the various stages of undertaking lesson studies in primary schools where the focus was on pupils with learning difficulties. All three cases indicate that the teachers involved in the Lesson Study projects gained from the experience, and that the pupils did make accelerated progress over a short period of time as indicated by teacher assessment. The teachers valued greatly the opportunity to plan lessons collaboratively, to carry out detailed observations of case pupils, to interview the pupils for their reflections on their learning, to have time to reflect on the research lessons and on their own learning and to see the progress children made. While unable to attribute the learning entirely to Lesson Study, all felt it had played a significant part. Head teachers in all cases had supported the project in their schools and were keen for these teachers to disseminate their knowledge to other staff and to explore ways of sustaining Lesson Study as an integral element of their professional development policy. Some of the specific aspects of these case studies will be discussed in more detail in the final chapter of this book.

5

Teachers' Lesson Study Practice in Secondary Schools

Di Hatchett

Introduction

In this chapter, I describe and analyse the work of practising teachers who participated in the 2010–12 University of Exeter Lesson Study-MLD project. The focus of this project, as explained in earlier chapters, was to research the potential of the Lesson Study approach in raising the attainment of students identified as having MLD. Another significant feature of this project was the creation of cross-subject specialism working by teachers in Key Stage 3 (early secondary year groups). These cases studies are informed by the case reports written by individual teachers who reported on their lesson studies. Background information about schools comes from Ofsted reports on the schools. These case reports were summaries of what had been done during the Lesson Studies and the outcomes of the Lesson Study cycles. As a consultant to these Lesson Study teams, I have drawn on these case reports and supplemented them with background information about the schools and the Lesson Study preparations to produce these illustrative case studies for this book. These case studies are presented as insider accounts of Lesson Studies by contrast to the external evaluative perspective on Lesson Studies in Chapter 6.

Case study 1

Context

This school is an average-sized secondary school and is non-selective within an area where selection operates in south-east England. The proportions of pupils identified as being in receipt of free school meals was below the national average. One in eight pupils were identified as having SEN, with the proportion of pupils with statements being double the national average. The Lesson Study team comprised a broad range of expertise and experience: assistant head teacher/director of science, art teacher, and a teacher who is second in the English department. This case study focused on the cycle of Lesson Study carried out in the English department.

The main aim of this Lesson Study was to improve the ability of students with MLD to explain a writer's purpose, recognize their target audience, and to be able to apply these skills to inform their own writing. The team also aimed to develop the pupils' confidence by enabling them to develop skills that would be transferrable to a range of lessons and different situations. A further aim was to develop pupils' vocabulary.

The purpose for the team was to make literacy lessons for pupils with learning difficulties more motivational and to develop the teacher's own capability to use language and resources appropriate to the pupils' needs. In conducting the Lesson Study, the team made use of various ideas and practices from relevant research:

1. 'Do supplemental remedial reading programs address the motivational issues of struggling readers? An analysis of five popular programs' (Quirk and Schwanenflugel, 2004).

Table 5.1 Background and starting levels of case pupil

Year 9 boy identified as having MLD and hearing impairment
Working at National Curriculum Level 3b in English
Finds it difficult to communicate his thoughts and ideas and has some difficulties interacting socially within the group
Can be very quiet and withdrawn in lessons
Does not actively seek help but will attempt to do something even if he is unclear about the task so as not to draw attention to himself
Aim for case pupil
Through Lesson Study to introduce strategies to help him develop his communication skills and thereby to increase his confidence and help him to be better integrated

2 *Cooperative reading as simple as ABC* (Raison, 2013).

3 *Raising boys' achievements in literacy* (Bearne, 2004).

Planning for research lesson 1

The team wanted the students to learn how to explain how different media texts appeal to an audience and to be able to apply this to their own writing. The idea was to use advertisements as media, as research showed that using small amounts of focused text with students with low literacy levels could be effective. It was also thought that looking at layout, use of image, colour and font, as well as the wording of the text, would be motivational and would help students think about the presentation of their own work. A combination of examples, paired work and individual work was used, as well as laptops to encourage children to write more freely and confidently.

Research lesson 1 and pupil observation and interviews

The English teacher taught the lesson while the other two members of the team observed the students and supported during the tasks. The case pupil was able to identify with very basic aspects like use of colour, but did not really progress beyond this. Pupils in the interview reported that they enjoyed the lesson and they liked being able to do their work on computers. They suggested that the lesson was a little bit too teacher-led and that they would have liked more time to complete activities. They liked the use of examples to explain the task and give them ideas, but felt too much time was spent on this. They also said that they found the tasks easy. They were disappointed not to have been able to complete the main task. The following are a selection of quotes from some of the children:

> It was fun, we got to go on computers, we don't normally get to go on computers in extra English, normally it's all books.
>
> We didn't get to finish which I thought was a little disappointing because it was fun.
>
> I think Miss should have just told us what to do and let us get on with it, then we would have more time to do it. I was in the middle of doing mine and didn't have enough time to finish.

Post-research lesson 1 discussion and planning research lesson 2

In this post-lesson discussion, the teachers considered that the use of adverts had been successful in engaging the children and they had responded well to the lesson. However, they felt that their expectations had been a bit low and that the lesson was not sufficiently challenging. They also felt that the children were explaining on a very basic, superficial level and were not really analysing the content, even though the teacher had tried to prompt this in the paired task.

For research lesson 2, they therefore decided to model how to analyse an advert, emphasizing useful words and phrases that the children could use in their analysis. Peer assessment of the work they had done in lesson 1 was to be introduced, so that pupils could analyse each other's adverts and suggest ways that they could be improved. Students would then be given a chance to improve their adverts from the previous lesson.

Research lesson 2

The aim was for the students to learn how to analyse an advert and then apply what they had learned to their own adverts. Teaching involved modelling how to analyse an advert and how to use that to inform making an advert. Peer assessment was used so that pupils could practise analysing adverts, while also learning how to improve their work. The intention was then for the students to use the skills they had developed to improve the adverts they had started in the previous lesson, as it was clearly important to them to have the opportunity to finish the work to the best of their ability.

The English teacher taught the lesson, but the other two teachers presented an analysis of an advert and a new advert created from thinking about the analysis. When not teaching, members of the team were observing the students. They noted that the students responded really well to the tasks. They liked the element of choice and creativity and were very engaged in the lesson.

The case pupil made good progress and showed better understanding of what was required of him. It was found that he was able to express himself much better orally, though his poor writing and spelling skills made him reluctant to write anything that was not very basic.

In interviews, the students said that they enjoyed the variety of tasks and found the peer assessment particularly useful. They had a clear understanding of what was expected of them and were clearer about what they had learnt. Quotes from students included the following:

I liked this lesson because it was more fun, a lot more things to do and we got to do our own stuff which was pretty cool.

I thought it was useful because you sort of walked us through it stage by stage and we knew how to do it.

I thought it was good that we could look at other people's work and see how we could improve ours and help them improve theirs.

I learnt how people who advertise lay stuff out on the page and who they aim stuff at.

I learnt how to make advertising better instead of just getting a picture and saying what it is. How to add more text and make it more appealing to other people and stuff like that.

Post-research lesson 2 discussion and planning for research lesson 3

Following analysis of how research lesson 2 went, it was decided that the aim for research lesson 3 was for pupils to learn how to analyse in more depth and how to expand their vocabulary to express their ideas in a more formal way. So, research lesson 3 was planned to start off by giving them a more complicated advert to annotate with sentence starters and a vocabulary list to help them write in a more analytical way. Peer assessment was to be continued as the pupils found this particularly useful. It was also decided to pair up the case pupil with a pupil who had a visual impairment and get them to use a voice recorder to make their comments so that they could develop their analytical and language skills without the threat of writing.

Post-research lesson 3 discussion

The English teacher taught the lesson, while the other members of the team observed the students. In the post-lesson discussion the team concluded that while there had been some success in making the lessons more motivational with pupils' interest being aroused, and there had been much progress in their participation and oral answers, their written analysis was still very superficial. Despite this, pupils were much better at recognizing the target audience and understanding how to make their own work appeal to a target audience; they made good use of colour, layout and font but still needed to make better use of text. However, the use of the voice recorder was not as successful as we had hoped because the case pupil felt self-conscious using it.

Impact of Lesson Study

The following quotes capture teachers' and some students' evaluation of the effects of the Lesson Study.

On pupil learning and progress

Quotes from pupils:

> It's nice to do something different.
> I liked these lessons and I've learnt a lot from them.
> I think I have improved some of my skills in literacy.
> I think I have improved quite a bit.
> I think I have become a bit more confident.

From a teacher:

> Using this approach, pupils with learning difficulties . . . will be better able to improve their literacy skills because they are more motivated, more confident and keener to participate. They were able to see the skills in a different context with relevancy to them. Introducing the use of computers in these lessons also made the pupils see that literacy isn't just about books and made them much more willing to engage and have a go at the tasks. Hopefully the literacy teacher, who observed the lessons, will see that the pupils can be motivated and engaged and eager to learn when they are presented with a variety of tasks and a different approach.

On teaching practice

> It encouraged us to have higher expectations of pupils with learning difficulties . . . and showed us the importance of trying to stretch these pupils. We started to learn how to challenge them with achievable goals and we would like to continue to develop this area.

On departmental and school approaches to teaching, learning, support for pupils with MLD and continuing professional development (CPD):

> We will continue to use Lesson Study as an approach to CPD within our school improvement strategy to help raise standards of teaching and learning in the school. We found staff working together in this way were able to experiment

with confidence and were more inspired. Involving the children in giving feedback was invaluable and really helped to improve the lessons and generate new ideas. It was also very motivating for the students.

Focusing on . . . a number of pupils with learning difficulties helped us to think more about how to challenge these students while still building their confidence. Encouraging other staff to have higher expectations of these students and what they can achieve will be an important impact of the Lesson Study process.

The school leadership team sees Lesson Study as a significant tool in school improvement and staff development.

Personal reflections

Lesson Study encouraged me to be much more reflective in my teaching and to appreciate how useful it is to involve students in their own learning. I really enjoyed working with colleagues in other departments and realized how beneficial collaboration can be. I also developed many different specific approaches to help students develop particular skills, for example:

- Teacher modelling
- Discovering that by developing pupils' skills rather than focusing on subject content they are able to develop better as independent learners and therefore their learning increases.

Case study 2

Context and aims

This school is an average-sized secondary school of about 1000 pupils, serving an area of significant economic and social deprivation in south-west England. The proportion of pupils identified as having SEN (36 per cent) was above the national average and the proportion entitled to free school meals (30 per cent) was significantly above the national average.

The Lesson Study team: the identified group of teachers comprised a broad range of expertise and experience – a teacher of drama (early in her career); head of art department; SENCo.

This case study focuses on the cycle of Lesson Study carried out in the art department. The team identified that in art pupils needed to be able to think deeply to make sophisticated connections and also to have the confidence and emotional literacy to be able to articulate their thoughts and feelings. They also wanted to improve the way pupils with MLD were able to demonstrate their understanding of concepts and develop higher-order thinking skills. In addition, they wanted to improve the way pupils with MLD were able to be aware of their feelings and discuss them with others. So their key areas of focus were higher-order thinking skills and developing emotional literacy.

They used Robert Fisher's papers on thinking skills, as their focus was higher-order thinking and metacognition; promoting pupils to reflect on their thinking and decision making process (Fisher, 2006). The team also used the TDA (2009) MLD advice on working with MLD students where pictures, words and feelings are used to support learning.

Teaching expertise was used to support emotional intelligence, by which the team meant 'a person's ability to assess and manage the emotions of one's self, of others, and of groups' (Goleman, 1995).

Planning for research lesson 1

In this lesson, the aim was develop emotional intelligence (defined as 'a person's ability to assess and manage the emotions of one's self, of others and of groups') in order to create a safe environment for students to deal with abstract concepts where there is no right or wrong answer.

Table 5.2 Background and starting levels of case pupil A and B

Pupil A	Pupil B
Was a quiet boy with good skill base working just below expectations in English and maths for his age group	Is a lively boy keen to offer suggestions and fit in with his peers
Had significant confidence issues and is reluctant to be an active participant in lessons	Was confident socially in making connections
	His work presented as scruffy and limited in depth
Aim for case pupil A	**Aim for case pupil B**
To focus on supporting this student's independent thinking, confidence, and active participation	To support him to develop higher-level thinking and stay focused on task

In this lesson, the students were asked to connect shapes and colours to feelings, they were also asked to record how they felt using colours. This was part of a broader scheme of work which looks at creating a composition that uses the concept of abstraction to reflect on a piece of music.

Research lesson 1

Having teachers focus their observations on individual students using film, audio and note-taking meant that the quality of observation was very detailed and precise. The class teacher was able to manage the whole class and deliver the planned lesson while also observing differences in the performance of the whole class.

Post-research lesson 1 discussion and planning research lesson 2

The post-lesson discussion showed that there were aspects of learning that the class teacher was not aware of, in particular the case pupils' responses. Based on the observation recorded in Table 5.3, the team realized that teacher assessment had historically put pupil A at a higher level because his sketchbook

Table 5.3 Observations of case pupils in research lesson 1

Pupil A	Pupil B
Relied heavily on copying	He had understood concepts and had been able to make connections between colours and shapes
Although the quality of the work looked good, he had developed a masking strategy	So could give reasoned answers to his decisions. For example, wavy lines being relaxed and black being dark and angry
This meant he did not have to generate ideas himself	But, rushed at the end due to worrying about finishing, resulting in using the same colour to describe everything
	Had developed a strategy whereby he wanted to finish a task rather than be confident enough to leave it unfinished but of better quality

looked better and B at a lower level, because his work looked scruffy and not thought through.

As a result of these findings the team decided to look at higher-level thinking skills and give the students a further opportunity to demonstrate and reflect on their own learning. As they were now more aware of how these pupils learned, it was felt that they needed to develop metacognitive skills. If they could develop an awareness of how they learned and exceed their own expectations, this should improve their achievement. This is where Fisher's (2006) ideas about thinking skills were used and the TDA (2009) advice about teaching pupils with MLD, as assisted by the SEN Coordinator.

Research lesson 2

In this lesson the pupils were learning about the artist Kandinsky. They were asked to build a picture of the kind of person Kandinsky was and work out as much as they could about him based on visual clues. They were given a starter activity as a whole class, which modelled the approach. They were then asked to work in pairs because it was felt that larger groups would be too intimidating for the case pupils. An envelope was given to each pair and students were asked to pull out clues and discuss. The same roles were kept as in research

Table 5.4 Research lesson 2 observations of case pupils

Pupil A	Pupil B
He was actively participating and listening in lessons	Engaged in deeper thinking in his pair work i.e., when looking at the Nazi symbol he thought Kandinsky may be a Nazi
But he was still relying heavily on his partner to come up with ideas first	His partner encouraged him to question and find out whether Kandinsky was a Russian maybe for or against the Nazi regime
	Working as a pair in a less linear approach was encouraging him to make deeper connections
	He took time to settle at first, took longer to fully engage in the lesson and was seeking attention from his peers a lot

lesson 1, with the rest of the team observing while the class teacher taught the planned lesson.

Post-research lesson 2 discussion

During the post-lesson discussion it was concluded that all students were engaged in making deeper connections and were actively participating in the task. The class teacher concluded that the whole class was more engaged than they had been with the previous method of introducing an artist using an information handout sheet and a Powerpoint presentation. When asked a few weeks later what they remembered about the artist Kandinsky, they were able to discuss his interest in music and connection with Nazi Germany. It seemed that they had retained more information when connecting this with emotion, shape and action.

For research lesson 3 it was decided to look at finding ways to support pupil B to stay focused and sustain his work. It was also decided to design ways that would enable pupil A to volunteer his ideas first and thus discover for himself and for us what he was really capable of achieving.

Research lesson 3

In the third lesson the students were asked to perform a 'Brain Gym' (Brain Gym International, 2013) activity as a starter and a Kagan Time–Pair–Share activity (Kagan, 1989) as a plenary. The main activity was to listen to sections of music and record their responses to it. In this lesson the Lesson Study focus was to look at how the starter and plenary activities could contribute to the achievements of the case pupils in the main activity. In this lesson the team drew on the SEN coordinator's experience of working with students with learning difficulties and Brain Gym and the drama teacher's experience with Kagan approaches that have been developed in the drama department.

As with the other two lessons, the art teacher led the lesson, with the other teachers observing pupils A and B.

Post-research lesson 3 discussion

It was concluded that allowing students to stand and be physical seemed to create a more settled start for all students. Pupil A learned that what he had to say was of value and so built his confidence; he felt safe in the pair and benefitted from not being given a choice about responding first.

Table 5.5 Observation of pupils A and B in research lesson 3

Pupil A	Pupil B
Seemed to need a break before engaging in the main activity	During the Time–Pair–Share activity, teacher arranged that he go first (by saying boy with longest hair go first)
But after the Brain Gym starter settled quickly into the main activity and was much more settled overall	He looked shocked at first, but had enough confidence to then contribute his thoughts about Kandinsky picture by Kandinsky projected on the whiteboard
	A time limit was given and then his partner shared his thoughts

Although each research lesson was reviewed separately, the general view of the team was that the emotional intelligence work had enabled pupils to feel safe to share ideas, with the use of higher-level thinking skills giving them confidence to achieve at a higher level. It was also observed that understanding from the whole group improved, with evidence from their sketchbooks showing higher-quality responses.

Impact of Lesson Study

The following quotes from the case report capture teachers' evaluation of the effects of the Lesson Study:

On pupil learning and progress

- Pupils who have lower than average literacy will be better able to understand contextual and critical studies because of a more multi-sensory approach that is not reliant on text.
- Pupils who do not have the confidence to volunteer information will have more opportunities to build confidence and share ideas through the exploration of Kagan techniques.
- Pupils will have increased awareness of themselves, their own learning and how they relate to others through the use of emotional learning strategies.

Impact on teaching practice:

> As a result of Lesson Study the art department intends to use the multi-sensory approach to critical studies when introducing artists at Key Stage 3. The department can develop strategies that reflect an awareness that a reliance on words and listening is not the best way to help students remember and understand broader concepts. Lesson Study has also been useful in helping us to identify two of the masking strategies that MLD students had been using to disguise their difficulties; i.e. copying and rushing to finish.

Impact on departmental and school approaches to teaching, learning and support for pupils with MLD and CPD:

- For MLD students multi-sensory approaches are essential;
- Reflections and processing time needs to be built in;
- Strategies where MLD students are given the opportunity to volunteer information first are manufactured;
- An awareness of their own abilities and learning needs to be developed through emotional intelligence strategies providing a safe context within which to reflect and volunteer ideas;
- Brain Gym activities were very effective in focusing learning;
- Changes in practice and teacher learning;
- Shared lesson planning is a very effective process;
- Focusing observation on students rather than teachers enables greater insights into the impact of teaching on learning;
- As a school we are intending to continue with the Lesson Study process as part of our whole school INSET programme where staff are divided into teaching and learning communities.

Personal reflections:

> Lesson Study focuses on the impact of the learner rather than the performance of the teacher. Through co-planning all adults involved are committed to and immersed in the process; the lead teacher is able to approach the dynamic of learning in a more creative way. The impact is significant on pedagogy and practice through reflection and collaboration.

Lesson Study reinforces what teachers come to work for every day: learning and teaching. Lesson Study keeps learning at the heart of all we do. I believe the very best lessons taught in schools allow students the space to explore their learning and the scope to make mistakes and take risks – the exact same applies to teachers. The more teachers explore, research, observe, discuss and take risks – the more profound the learning experience for the students. Lesson Study supports this like no other professional development opportunity. Lesson Study takes place at the heart of the school in the classroom; it is empowering for both teachers and students.

Case study 3

Context and aims

This school is a large secondary school of 1500 pupils serving a diverse area of a city in south-west England. The proportions of pupils identified as having SEN and in receipt of free school meals were above national averages. The school was an accredited specialist college for mathematics and computing. It also had a designated unit for pupils with visual impairment. The Lesson Study team was appointed following an internal process of advertisement and application. It comprised the Key Stage 3 manager for English and the faculty leader for creative industries. This case study focuses on the cycle of Lesson Study carried out in the English department.

The team chose to focus on developing students' reading responses, as this was such a significant area of their English curriculum throughout the school. Students often struggled to construct higher-level analysis in formulating responses to reading (in keeping with the principles of PEEL paragraphs Point, Explain, Example and Link). This is a crucial aspect for attaining higher grades at GCSE, so they wanted to explore new avenues and methods of making this process more accessible and enjoyable for students. In particular, they wanted to improve the way the pupils with MLD, and in fact all of their students, learn about how to identify, explore and comment on the writer's craft within a prose text.

The team also researched the idea of collaborative learning through resources such as *The Red Book of Groups: and how to lead them better* (Houston, 1984) and pedagogical practice ideas from *Creative thinking in literacy, art and design* (National Strategies/DCSF, 2002).

Table 5.6 Background and starting levels of case pupil A and B

Pupil A	Pupil B
Had been identified as having MLD	Had been identified as having MLD
Always appeared keen and engaged, but failed to create higher-level responses	Demonstrated issues of engagement during lessons and often settled for presenting initial ideas, without challenging himself further
Aims for both pupils	
To enjoy the lessons while also developing their understanding and ability to construct higher-level responses to what they read	

Research lesson 1 and case pupil interviews

The aim in the first lesson was for pupils to have an overall understanding of the Prologue to *Romeo and Juliet* in which the Chorus introduces the conflict between the two families involved. The objective was for pupils to be able to explore how tension is created and to identify and explore the effectiveness of various language techniques. Students had a copy of the Prologue, along with some shadow puppets for them to re-create the story. They were then given a pack of weapons, each of which had a different language technique written on it. They had to find examples of the techniques within the text and attach them to the weapons using sticky tack. Then they had to create an order of effectiveness of these techniques by deciding which weapon they would use to attack different parts of a samurai silhouette (e.g. which technique could be used to most effectively/fatally attack a particular area of the body, such as his head or heart). Students were asked to justify their choices.

Pupils reported in their interviews at the end of the research lesson that they really enjoyed the tactile nature of the tasks. There was also evidence that they were actively trying to select and order their ideas (weapons) in line with which parts of the text they found more effective. However, observations showed that they did not focus on the detail of the text in this activity.

Post-research lesson 1 discussion and planning research lesson 2

Analysis and discussion of observations that the case pupils did not focus on the detail of the text in the shadow puppet activity led to the decision that this would be the area of focus for research lesson 2. To address this issue of 'textual focus', the plan was to encourage students to read the text more closely by dividing it up into colour-coded sections, and by giving each pair a section to mime. This was to be done by introducing an element of challenge by asking the students to guess which section was being performed.

Research lesson 2

When introduced in research lesson 2 this activity worked really well: students were commenting on particular parts of the text to justify why they thought the performance was that colour, e.g. it says 'he lowered his guard' so it must be the blue section.

As the use of weapons had been really successful in the last lesson, it was decided to introduce the idea of ninja stars for the students to write on. So, after the teacher had discussed and explored what a PEEL paragraph was, students selected a weapon and used that to create a point on one of the tips of the stars. They then had to select some evidence for the point to write on the next tip. Then they had to describe the effect of that evidence on the third one and explain how it created tension for the reader on the fourth tip.

Post-research lesson 2 discussion and planning research lesson 3

In the post-lesson discussion, the Lesson Study team observations were compared and analysed. These confirmed that the case pupils had found the describing of the point and explaining how this created tension quite challenging. So it was decided to examine how to support explanations in the next lesson. Observations had also shown that the case pupils were more comfortable in tackling this challenging task collaboratively in groups. During the feedback process, the PEEL paragraphs were seen as a group outcome and were not personalized to individuals; this made discussion about the activity more honest and constructive. Analysis of the final activity of research lesson 2 was also revealing. This activity involved identifying the positive aspects of another group's PEEL paragraph by comparing it to the criteria in the prompt cards (to enable higher-level explanations). It was observed that this boosted confidence and the case pupils subsequently reported that they felt less concerned and anxious about their end of unit Assessment of Pupil Progress (APP) on another section of the samurai text.

Research lesson 3

The third lesson started with a samurai-shaped sorting activity, which enabled the pupils to be exposed to a wider range of model examples and consolidate their understanding of how to structure a PEEL paragraph. The majority of pupils were able to use the activity as a point of discussion to explore what makes a good PEEL paragraph.

Students were then given further ninja stars, along with some interview prompt cards to support them in a ninja star consequences activity. The pupils would pick a different weapon to the previous lesson and use it to write a point about it on the tip of their stars. Then they would pass it along to their neighbour, who would select some textual evidence to support it. Before the third and fourth points were written, pupils would use the 'explain and link' prompt cards to rehearse their explanations through talk before writing them down. They would also discuss their ideas before committing it to the star. As each star was a collaborative effort, pupils would be more willing to read them out, discuss them (without offending a friend) and offer constructive comments (linked to the prompt cards) about how to improve them and ensure they offered more detailed explanations. The final activity was to take a different weapon again and create, rehearse and then commit a final PEEL paragraph on to a coloured samurai or ninja cut-out. These were finally displayed on the wall to effectively create a continuous text.

Post-research lesson 3 discussion

After this lesson, teachers in the team felt overall that they had learned that using the prompt cards as a checklist was important, as otherwise the pupils often settled for their initial ideas. The prompt cards and rehearsal time enabled them to amend and extend thinking beyond their first idea.

Impact of Lesson Study

The following quotes from the case report capture teachers' evaluation of the effects of this Lesson Study.

On pupil learning and progress:

> Pupils who have MLD will be better able to learn how to develop reading responses if they are able to practise constructing example paragraphs collaboratively in groups, given rehearsal time before committing their ideas to paper, given prompt cards to structure and support their discussions, given exciting tactile resources to handle (and develop ownership), allowed to write on an interesting shape and not in their exercise books (shapes can be stuck in to provide evidence) and engaged initially by challenges and 'fun' tasks.

On teaching practice:

> I will never teach students how to form a reading response in the same way. I will always use the collaborative 'consequences style' approach when developing student ability to construct their paragraphs, as the PEEL assessment discussion is less personal and students feel more comfortable, to give honest and constructive comment. The prompt cards for developing higher-level explanations and links were useful during the talk rehearsal time and when evaluating the quality of a PEEL paragraph. Rehearsal time is another element which I will include as it is a strategy to encourage students to not just accept their initial idea, but develop it further before writing it down.
>
> I will also consolidate the use of activities to support students in starting the process. Artefacts used can always be stuck in books to provide evidence of drafting.

On departmental and school approaches to teaching, learning, support for pupils with MLD and CPD:

> We have already delivered a CPD session on Lesson Study, as well as presenting our studies so far to curriculum managers at the college and have generated a really positive and enthusiastic response.
>
> Next steps will be to develop a Lesson Study group, as part of our whole-college CPD. Ideally, we will share our case studies and experiences before offering to act as coaches to new colleagues who are passionate and keen to become involved. We aim to establish an interactive Lesson Study site in our shared network area, where staff can share their findings via a summative evaluative Powerpoint presentation or even a short video.

Personal reflections:

- Completely changed our practice and perception of teaching. Our fuel for teaching has been re-ignited!
- Embedded new skills to deliver literacy, creativity and group work into our practice and our departments and whole school – due to cascading our new knowledge and resources through CPD sessions.
- We both feel more confident to be innovative and take more risks within our lessons.
- This has raised our standing within the school and we are seen as a source of expertise within school.

Case study 4

Context

This is a larger-than-average-sized secondary school with a language specialism serving a wide catchment area in south-west England. The proportion of pupils known to be eligible for free school meals was below the national average while pupils identified as having SEN, including those with Statements, was above the national average. The Lesson Study team comprised the school's SEN coordinator, a teacher from the English department and a teacher from the history department. All those involved were experienced teachers with specific interests in supporting pupils identified as having SEN.

The focus of the Lesson Study was a year 8 English unit on media. Part of this involved analysing the humour used in an episode of *The Simpsons*. The team chose this focus as the unit of work was current and the class in question contained a number of pupils with MLD, making it an appropriate choice for this project.

An overall aim was to improve behaviour for learning and promote independent learning, by using the school's recently introduced Virtual Learning Environment (VLE).

In conducting the Lesson Study, the team members drew on their own professional knowledge and expertise, particularly that of the SENCo in terms of a wide range of strategies to use with pupils with MLD. The team also consulted the following literature:

- The Lamb Inquiry (DCSF, 2009) which suggested that the students would make more progress if they could interact with the teachers, not just the teaching assistants (TAs). In the Lesson Study they planned for this by using the VLE to engage all pupils – the teacher could spend time with pupils with MLD who might otherwise have been overlooked.

- Gathercole and Alloway (2008): ideas from working memory research suggested that lessons should be structured so that pupils did not have to remember too much at once. This was achieved by having all the verbal instructions repeated on the VLE. The research also suggested that pupils do well when they have a range of enjoyable ways to consolidate new knowledge – the lessons were built around comedy clips on the VLE – providing an interesting way for pupils to consolidate learning.
- Fletcher-Campbell (2004) confirmed that pupils with MLD would be able to follow a programme of work broadly similar to their peers. In our Lesson Study, a similar scheme was followed for all pupils – so there was no need for pupils to have a completely separate activity.

Planning for research lesson 1

The team wanted students to gain an understanding of different types of humour in order to provide a basis for future lessons. The approach used was based on the school's VLE because it was felt that the use of this would provide a vehicle for independent learning and it would support pupils with MLD by using text-to-speech software to help them access the text. The use of audiovisual (AV) clips would also aid pupil understanding – by providing real-life examples of types of humour.

Table 5.7 Background and starting levels of case pupils

Pupil A	Pupil B	Pupil C
Year 8, identified as having MLD	Year 8, identified as having specific learning difficulties	Year 8, overall lower attaining
Largely passive in lessons supported by TA and reliant on this support	Works independently and can work at higher levels	Disruptive behaviour in lessons and lack of commitment to tasks

Research lesson 1 and pupil observation and interviews

The English teacher taught the lesson with the other two members of the team observing the class with a focus on individual students. All staff provided support to pupils during the lesson. Their observations noted the following:

- Pupils with MLD were working outside their comfort zones – they could not rely on traditional coping strategies – e.g. teaching assistant, teacher, peer support. This encouraged them to work independently and most of the case pupils did make progress.
- The activities were engaging and provided for a range of learning preferences (virtual, auditory).
- Impact on behaviour for learning was marked – and significantly improved. The lesson took place during the last period of the day; in previous weeks pupil behaviour had deteriorated, impacting on learning. The use of headphones and engaging tasks meant that pupils were focused and off-task behaviour, e.g. calling out, was minimized.

The team had recorded positive responses by pupils who had appreciated the change from the 'usual routine' and that distractions were minimized. Pupils had also said that they liked being able to watch the clips several times as this had helped them to match the clips to the definitions.

Post-research lesson 1 discussion and planning research lesson 2

In this post-lesson discussion the team noted that there had been issues with the Information and Communication Technology (ICT) equipment not working properly, so they needed to ensure this did not obstruct future lesson delivery. They also agreed that the wording used on the worksheet (definitions of humour) had not been sufficiently differentiated. As a result, the wording to be used in lesson 2 was further differentiated and more precisely matched to the clips the pupils would be watching. The team also planned to match the questions more specifically to each AV clip in order to help the pupils focus more precisely.

Planning for research lesson 2

The team wanted students to develop skim-and-scan techniques as this was a skill many had struggled with previously. Poor research skills had been identified generally as an across-curriculum issue in the school. This was the subject of a special interest group in the school.

Originally the team had planned to use the VLE in order to facilitate individual and independent learning. However, the software would not work with the particular website they wanted to use and they were concerned about potential distractions on the website. As a result, the team decided to print information and have pupils work in groups to skim-and-scan. This also provided a balance to research lesson 1 which, on further reflection, the team concluded, had provided limited opportunity for pupil talk.

Research lesson 2 pupil observations and interviews and post-lesson discussion

The SENCo taught the lesson with the other two members of the team observing the class with a focus on individual students. All staff provided support to pupils during the lesson. The team was keen to encourage the participation of *all* pupils in the group task and achieved this by giving each pupil in the group a different coloured pen. This was to encourage them to contribute to the group and record their findings on the sheet provided.

In post-lesson interviews, pupils said they liked the group work and the choice to share new information about well-known characters from *The Simpsons* with the rest of the group. Content-wise, the team felt that the lesson had been successful. In terms of pupil skills, they did use skim-and-scan, although some of the pupils with MLD and other SEN struggled to identify key information about the characters and needed prompting to do this.

Planning research lesson 3

The team aimed for pupils to use their prior learning to analyse the types of humour used in an episode of *The Simpsons*. This lesson was informed more by research lesson 1 than research lesson 2, as it was again based on using the VLE in the computer rooms.

Research lesson 3 pupil observations and interviews

The English teacher taught the lesson, and the other teachers again observed individual pupils. This lesson worked better from a technical point of view – students were familiar with the VLE and the structure of the lesson. The team noted that fewer pupils asked for help – showing that the specific questions had worked more effectively in terms of guiding pupils to what they had to do, and focusing them on the key points the team had wanted them to learn from each clip.

In interviews pupils said they did not like having to switch between the clips and writing their answers, but only two had taken the option of writing on paper, which would have avoided the need to do this. All agreed that they had achieved more in this lesson (which took place in the second period on Monday) than in previous afternoon lessons, during which poor behaviour had become a pattern.

Research lesson 3 post-lesson discussion

In this discussion, the team identified some key issues.

- They had labelled some questions as 'harder questions' thinking that doing these would boost self-esteem when pupils realized they could do them. However, many pupils were put off by this label; asking whether they 'had to do this'. On reflection this raised questions of pupils' ambition and unwillingness to experience potential failure.
- Despite step-by-step instructions being available on the screen, some pupils still asked for help rather than reading the instructions. It appeared that this, for some pupils, was learned behaviour and an automatic response. This reflected a concern raised in the Lamb Report (DCSF, 2009).
- Pupil C was very negative about the questions – reluctant to write answers and assuming that he would not be able to do them. The teacher encouraged him and the fact that everyone else was on task meant there were no alternatives. Normally he would distract others and avoid work by behaving poorly. This normal peer group were sitting away from him and were working, so in the end he did too and once started did well, encouraging him to continue and do more questions.

Impact of Lesson Study

Some conclusions about teaching and learning, using the VLE and on the need to promote independent learning:

- Positive effect of the VLE on behaviour for learning.
- Usefulness of the VLE to differentiate learning resources in a way that is not obvious.

- Need to balance ICT–VLE lessons with opportunities to discuss and work in groups.
- Greater focus on differentiation and the level of differentiation needed in lessons.
- Independent learning will be a key feature of lessons in future – to maximize the progress that each student makes.
- Using the VLE effectively will enable pupils to have greater control of their own learning.

On departmental and school approaches to teaching, learning, support for pupils with MLD and continuing professional development:

- There was a shift in focus from the teacher and teaching to the students and their learning.
- There were benefits to working collaboratively across departments.
- Need to manage the role of teaching assistants in class to maximize learning of pupils with MLD/SEN:
  - ➢ Talking before the lesson about key objectives,
  - ➢ Need to encourage independence in pupils.
- During lessons teacher will be more aware of coping strategies used by pupils with MLD/SEN.
- Planning will be collaborative in future, whenever possible, and this was a real benefit of the Lesson Study. This will have an impact on the department's approach to curriculum development.
- An assistant principal has been involved in the Lesson Study and is keen to take the approach forward.
- Lessons learnt will be shared with all staff at a future Twilight Session on differentiation.
- Our VLE pages will be used as an example during the VLE training of other staff.

Personal reflection:

> It has been a valuable experience – watching other teachers teach across subjects has given me lots of new ideas about teaching and learning and has raised important issues which need to be considered.

The collaborative nature of the planning and evaluation has been great. The lessons developed as a result have been very effective in terms of pupils' learning. Even when they didn't go to plan we have learnt a lot from them.

The project has encouraged reflection within the department which otherwise wouldn't have taken place. The lesson observations are less threatening than traditional observations. The focus on pupils, not teachers, is valuable.

Concluding comments

These four case studies are illustrative of common themes and findings across the 30 schools involved in the Lesson Study-MLD project:

- A range of evidence shows that the case pupils' engagement and learning were enhanced.
- Engaging with the Lesson Study process resulted in new perspectives for the teachers involved in terms of the dynamics of teaching and learning in the classroom and, often, a renewed enthusiasm for teaching as a profession.
- Teachers found the experience of collaborative lesson planning and debriefing with colleagues from other subject disciplines to be refreshing, stimulating and pedagogically highly productive as teaching techniques were shared and joint research undertaken.
- The focus upon the close observation of case pupils resulted in new insights into the responses of pupils with MLD to classroom teaching and the ways in which they function during tasks and activities. In its turn, this led to the introduction of enhanced pedagogical approaches to support the learning of these pupils, which also proved of benefit to pupils in the class as a whole.
- These case studies show how various kinds of knowledge and practical guidance from various sources were used in the Lesson Study process.
- The involvement of senior school leaders, whether as part of the Lesson Study team or as supporters of the process, was pivotal for schools to gain the most from involvement in the project and enable the school to capitalize on the experience and teacher learning longer term.

The wider evaluation of the lesson studies and its consequences are analysed in the next chapter, which summarizes the findings of the evaluation wing of the project overall. Some of the specific aspects of these case studies will also be discussed in more detail in the final chapter.

PART THREE

Lesson Study Evaluation: Ways Forward

The last two chapters take a broader and integrative perspective about Lesson Study theory, practice and research. Chapter 6 draws together the outcomes of the evaluation research undertaken in the evaluation wing of the Lesson Study-MLD project. Chapter 7 examines what has been learned about how Lesson Study makes a difference to teaching pupils with learning difficulties and concludes with a summary of future prospects and ways forward.

6

Lessons from Evaluations of Lesson Study

Annamari Ylonen and Brahm Norwich

Introduction

In this chapter, we outline and summarize the main research findings of the Lesson Study-MLD Project, as well as their wider research implications. We begin with a brief look at the kinds of research approaches that have been used to examine the Lesson Study process internationally, mainly in the United States, before summarizing the specific research methods and their rationales used in the Lesson Study-MLD project. In the following five sections of the chapter, we then discuss the main facets and findings of this research.

In Phase 1 of the project (2010–2011), the main areas of evaluation were related to the following three areas: first, the category of MLD; second, teachers' views about MLD and teaching strategies developed for pupils with MLD; and third, a process evaluation of Lesson Study focusing on the contexts, mechanisms and outcomes.

In Phase 2 (2011–2012), the main two facets of research were first, the evaluation of outcomes of the Lesson Study process on the case pupils who had been identified with MLD, and second, ethnographic research in a small number of schools where observations were carried out and interviews undertaken. We conclude the chapter with a summary of the research findings from the five broad research strands and highlight the significance of this research.

In the first section we start off by discussing the different types of research approaches that can be used to examine the Lesson Study process, the challenges involved when researching Lesson Study, and the research approaches that we used in this project. In the next section we examine the main research findings of the five strands of research as outlined above and their implications. Finally, in the last section we draw out some overall conclusions about the findings relating to the category of MLD and the Lesson Study process.

Approaches to researching Lesson Study

The Lesson Study process, and in particular how it can improve teaching and learning in schools, has attracted much practical and some empirical research attention. Much of this research, however, has not been directed towards examining the actual mechanisms that produce specific outcomes. It tends to focus on prescribing or describing, rather than systematically researching Lesson Study (Sibbald, 2009). Is there, then, any evidence about positive teaching and learning outcomes associated with Lesson Study? As discussed in Chapters 1 and 2, there is some research evidence that Lesson Study improves teaching through developing teachers' knowledge and professional collaboration that can enhance pupil learning (Lewis, 2009; Lewis *et al.*, 2009; Puchner and Taylor, 2006). Collaboration can enhance teacher efficacy, leading to improved pupil engagement and learning, on one hand, while teachers can acquire new insights and improve their teaching via participating in Lesson Study (Lee, 2008; Rock and Wilson, 2005).

In a national and international context, where research evidence is expected to justify educational practices (Hammersley, 2007), the question of whether Lesson Study 'works' is an important but in no way a simple question. Research by using Randomized Control Trials (RCT) is often considered as providing the most reliable type of research evidence because it involves the use of control groups, thus enabling comparisons to be made between those who have been undergone a programme like Lesson Study and those who have not. However, though the RCT design has its place in research approaches, its adoption reflects more the interests of the research producers than research users like teachers. Teachers are not only likely to be interested in whether an approach like Lesson Study *can* be efficacious in optimal conditions, but also whether the method is relevant to specific practice and what contextual factors may affect the outcomes (Cartwright, 2007; Cartwright and Stegenga, 2008).

We discussed in Chapter 1 the two different routes to researching school teaching improvements, by using a general proof route and a local proof route (see Chapter 1 for details). In this project, a local proof route approach was used because the use of Lesson Study in professional learning and teaching development is at an early stage, and because adopting Lesson Study as a strategy still needed to be defined in operational terms. There has been little Lesson Study use in the UK and none in the area of teaching pupils with learning difficulties and disabilities. A general proof route (with the use of RCTs) is more suited to interventions that are well-defined and where the intervention is less likely to interact with the context of its use. These conditions did not match the aims of this project, which were to refine the use of Lesson Study using a design-based research approach (Cobb *et al.*, 2003), while providing evidence from the particular use of Lesson Study to develop teaching approaches for pupils identified as having MLD.

Five major strands of evaluation research were undertaken within the scope of the Lesson Study-MLD project, which utilized different methodological approaches based on a local proof route. In the first phase of the project, these consisted of (1) an evaluation of the usefulness of the concept of MLD focusing on examining the participating pupils' reasoning and literacy using British Ability Scales (BAS) and their learning dispositions, and (2) survey questionnaires evaluating participating teachers' attitudes and beliefs about the concept of MLD and teaching strategies for MLD. In addition, we carried out Lesson Study process evaluation using a realist evaluation methodological approach, which is discussed in more detail below. Realistic Evaluation (RE) aims to link three distinct broad aspects of a programme: its context, mechanisms and outcomes (C-M-Os) by constructing a programme theory that explains what processes (mechanisms) under what conditions (contexts) result in what outcomes. What characterizes this evaluative approach is its realist ontological assumptions; in other words, that there are underlying causal mechanisms (a generative model of causation) triggered by specific context factors that produce various outcomes (Pawson and Tilley, 1997). It was this aspect of realist evaluation that is relevant to the local route proof approach used in this design-based evaluation of Lesson Study.

In phase 2 of the project (2011–2012), we focused on the two major strands of evaluation research. The first of these was set to analyse the outcomes of the Lesson Study process on the case pupils using a method called goal monitoring and evaluation, and the second used ethnographic research methods focusing in particular on observational and interviewing methods. We analyse and discuss the main findings of these research strands later in this chapter.

Research findings about the category of moderate learning difficulties

One of the main project aims was to evaluate the usefulness of the category of MLD. This research focused on three distinct areas:

1. How MLDs were identified in the project schools.
2. What the normative pattern of reasoning and literacy BAS scores were for pupils identified as having MLD and how these contrasted with other pupils not having MLD.
3. How these pupils' (identified as having MLD) academic self-concepts, attitudes to school and class and their resilience compared and contrasted with others.

The number of pupils in this study, including the pupils who had been identified with MLD and the contrast pupils from the same classes who had been identified with Specific Learning Difficulties (SpLD), low attaining and average attaining pupils are outlined in Table 6.1 (for an explanation of the SEN system in England, see Appendix A).

Table 6.1 Number and percentages of pupils in the study

Case pupils	Total number	%
Pupils with MLD (total)	61	51.3
Of whom 'School Action'	(22)	–
Of whom 'School Action plus'	(8)	–
Of whom 'Statement'	(12)	–
Unknown	(19)	–
Pupils with SpLD	25	21.0
Pupils who are low attaining	19	16.0
Pupils who are average attain.	14	11.8
Total	**119**	**100**

Measures and analysis

A short questionnaire was designed to find out how the schools identified pupils as having MLD. Five options were provided:

1. Low attainment only
2. Low attainment and low intellectual levels
3. As not having a specific learning difficulty nor severe learning difficulty

4 Do not know; identified by SEN staff/department

5 As specified on a Statement.

Participating teachers had to select the options that applied in their school. Out of the 14 schools that completed the Lesson Study in the first phase of the project, responses to the questionnaire were received from teachers at 12 schools. The instructions were for the teachers to consult the school's SEN coordinator in completing this questionnaire so that the responses reflected school identification practice.

All 119 pupils who took part in this research were assessed individually at the pupils' own school by two qualified educational researchers before the start of the lesson studies using a range of measures (see Table 6.2).

These measures were used to assess current intellectual functioning, current word-level literacy attainments and current learning-related dispositions. Intellectual functioning and literacy measures were selected because of their relevance to various conventional and historical indicators of MLD, while the dispositional measures are relevant to other associated aspects of MLD, such as self-esteem. While using the psychometric measures of intellectual functioning, we were aware that these cannot be interpreted as valid measures of intelligence. The participating pupils could under-perform on these scales, though the use of individual assessment and the building of personal rapport by the assessors made this less likely than group-based cognitive ability tests. We were also aware of the issues in interpreting scores in terms of national norms and that there is variability in cognitive scores over time. Nor did we assume that once-off scores indicate fixed level of intellectual functioning or potential.

Where norms were used to interpret BAS scores, this involved either using T-scale scores (scales with means of 50 and standard deviations of 10, or standard-scale scores with means of 100 and standard deviations of 15).

Results

It emerged that the project schools had varied ways to identify MLD. In some schools low attainment only was the basis for identification, while in others low attainment and low cognitive abilities was the basis. This finding is in line with the other UK studies about how MLDs are identified at local authority level (Norwich and Kelly, 2005; Frederickson and Cline, 2009). Though MLD is expected by government guidelines to be recorded only at School Action Plus and Statement levels, in some schools pupils who were recorded at School Action level were also identified as having MLD (see Appendix A for an explanation of the SEN system in England). Follow-up enquiries indicated that

Table 6.2 Measures used in assessing the concept of MLD

	Measures	Additional details
Reasoning	British Ability Scales II Matrices	Figural analogies
	British Ability Scales II Similarities	Verbal concepts
Literacy	British Abilities Scales II Word Reading Scales	Individual word reading
	British Abilities Scales II Spelling Scales	Individual word spelling
Dispositions	Learner self-concept: Myself-as-a Learner Scale (Burden, 2000)	Beliefs and evaluations about the self as a learner
	Resilience: The Mastery and Relatedness scales of the Resiliency scales (Prince-Embury, 2007)	Mastery: optimism; self-efficacy; adaptability. Relatedness: sense of trust; perceived access to support; comfort with others; tolerance of difference
	Attitudes to Class Learning and School	Two scales were developed using statements derived from research-based studies about pupil attitudes. Attitudes to class learning scales consisted of 5 statements (e.g. 'I avoid doing class work because it is too hard') (Cronbach's alpha from the current study = 0.77). Attitudes to school scales had 7 statements (e.g. 'I get enough help at school with learning') (Cronbach's alpha from the current study = 0.84).

teachers used the MLD category in some schools because pupils at School Action level of SEN were deemed to have MLD like those at School Action Plus. Also, School Action Plus is defined officially in terms of a pupil having SEN and having had some outside support service involvement. In some schools this kind of involvement was unavailable, so pupils may stay recorded as being at School Action level, when they might, were outside support available, be identified at School Action Plus. The fact that teachers in some schools reported that the SEN department identified pupils as having MLD also suggests that some teachers may not understand the practice of MLD identification. Overall, these findings provide further evidence that the concept of MLD in the English school system is used in different ways, which reflects the national definition of MLD that is loosely formulated and has no clear operational details.

The research findings about the normative position of those identified as having MLD in terms of reasoning and literacy levels showed the following. If reasoning scores below the second percentile are taken as indicating mild intellectual disability or MLD, then only 17 per cent of the MLD group in these schools were in this range (see Figure 6.1). Over half of the MLD group had reasoning scores in the below average/average ranges. This is consistent with the finding that in some schools MLD was not identified in terms of low cognitive abilities. It is also reflected in the finding that the mean reasoning scores for the MLD was just above 40 on T-scale, well above the T-scale score of 30 or second percentile. It is also notable that only those with MLD who had a Statement had reasoning scores at the T-scale 30 or second percentile level (see Figure 6.3). The majority of pupils identified as having MLD in these schools were at School Action and School Action Plus, with mean reasoning scores in the below average range; T-scale 40–50 range (see Norwich *et al.*, 2012 for more details).

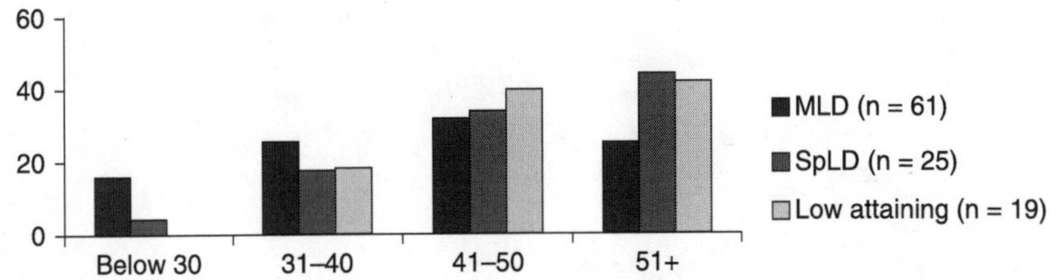

Figure 6.1 *Distribution of BAS reasoning T-scores for MLD, SpLD and low attaining pupils*

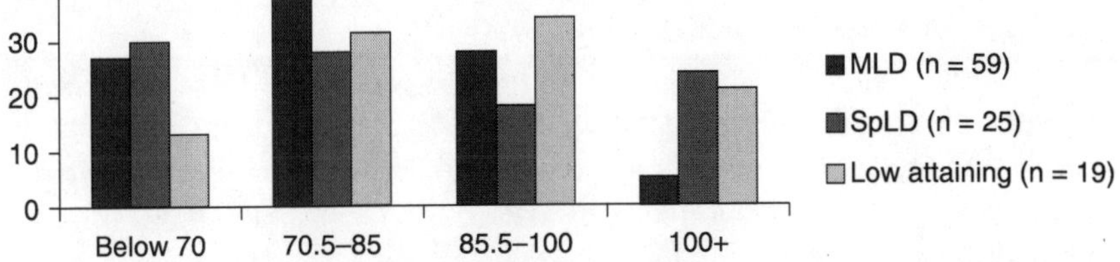

Figure 6.2 *Distribution of BAS literacy T-scores for MLD, SpLD and low attaining pupils*

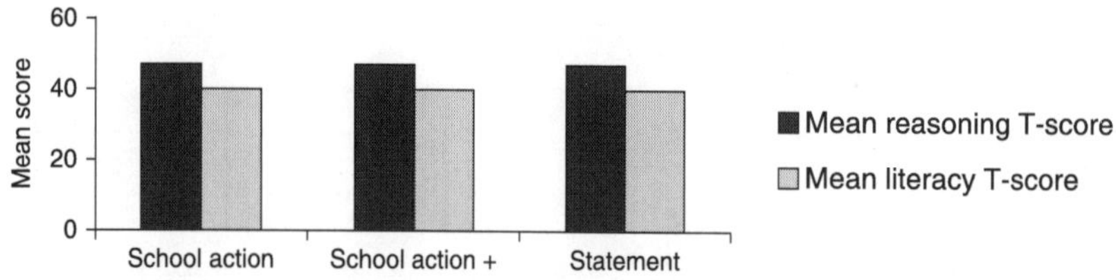

Figure 6.3 *Mean BAS reasoning and literacy T-scores for pupils with different levels of SEN*

Table 6.3 Average reasoning and literacy and difference scores for pupils with MLD by level of need

	MLD: School Action (n = 22)	MLD: School Action+ (n = 8)	MLD: statement (n = 12)	F-value (df)	Post hoc comparison
Average reasoning T-score (SD)	47.1 (9.9)	43.3 (8.8)	33.5 (7.1)	8.98 (2/41)**	SA>statement
Average literacy T-score (SD)	39.3 (6.0)	36.1 (7.8)	29.5 (11.0)	5.73 (2/40)**	SA>statement
Difference score (SD)	−7.7 (9.8)	−7.1 (5.9)	−5.2 (12.2)	0.24 (2/40) NS	

** p<0.01: NS, not significant

The mean literacy scores for the MLD group were much below their mean reasoning scores (see Figure 6.2). This was also shown in the finding that about 65 per cent of those identified with MLD had literacy scores below the T-scale level of 40 compared to about 42 per cent for reasoning scores. The fact that these pupils' literacy scores were much lower than their reasoning scores can be seen as consistent with the use of attainment in literacy as a basis for identifying MLD in the sample, especially for those at School Action and School Action Plus levels of SEN.

For the learning disposition scores, the only significant differences were between the specific learning difficulty group and the average group for school and class attitudes and resilience-relatedness. The MLD group did not differ from others without MLD in terms of their academic self-concepts, attitudes and resilience (see Norwich *et al.*, 2012).

The overall pattern of scores suggests that there is no basis for distinguishing between the MLD and the specific learning difficulties and low attaining groups in these schools (for an extended discussion and analysis, see Norwich *et al.*, 2012). These findings show uncertainty and important differences in how the MLD category is used in the project schools, which is reflected in the wide range of functioning for pupils identified as having MLD. If MLD is taken as equivalent to mild intellectual disabilities as used in health service classifications such as in the *Diagnostic and Statistical Manual* (DSM) (see Chapter 3 in this volume), then the study shows that only those identified as having MLD with Statements came close to meeting these criteria.

Teacher attitudes and teaching approaches for MLD

The research in this strand aimed to find out how the participating teachers interpreted the concept of MLD and whether the teachers developed and/or used MLD-specific teaching approaches while taking part in the project. In this chapter it is only possible to consider some of the findings of this research, which are relevant to the themes of this book (see Ylonen and Norwich, 2012 for an extended analysis including a discussion about teachers' self-efficacy and views about inclusion).

Two separate questionnaires were the main methods of collecting data in this strand of evaluation. The first questionnaire, focusing on teacher beliefs and attitudes, was designed to map the views of the participating teachers on different aspects of the concept of MLD. The statements about inclusion and MLD were designed for this study and based on previous theory and research about MLD (Norwich and Kelly, 2005). This survey was undertaken at the beginning of phase 1 of the project in November 2010 (completed by 34 teachers). The second questionnaire was designed to elicit from teachers at the end of phase 1 of the Lesson Study programme (July 2011) what specific teaching approaches and strategies they had used and developed through their Lesson Studies which focused on pupils with MLD as their case pupils (completed by 22 teachers).

Table 6.4 summarizes the findings about how the participating teachers perceived the concept of MLD. In this analysis, all unanswered questions were treated as 'not sure' answers. It can be seen that there was a low level of consensus about MLD, where consensus was defined as the percentage of responses above 70 per cent for agree or disagree and greater than 30 per cent for unsure responses. No aspect of MLD reached a consensus of more than 70 per cent, while all seven aspects of MLD had unsure responses higher than 30 per cent. This finding suggests that there was a prevailing uncertainty among many of the participating teachers about how to conceptualize MLD.

The responses show that the teachers were divided about the place of low intellectual abilities in defining MLD: while 44 per cent agreed that intellectual abilities are part of the definition of MLD, almost as many (41 per cent) were unsure. The responses to the statement whether MLD should not be regarded as an intellectual disability show that most teachers were unsure (56 per cent), while 35 per cent agreed. Most teachers saw MLD as not a specific learning difficulty or a severe learning difficulty, while most were unsure about the origins of MLD in social and familial disadvantage. Despite the majority of the teachers seeing MLD as not easily differentiated from low attainment and a majority being unsure about whether MLD should be regarded as an intellectual disability or not, it is interesting that only a minority agreed that the concept of MLD was problematic and should not be used (see Table 6.4).

Table 6.4 Teachers' concepts of MLD (percentages in bold are the modal responses), n = 34

Frequencies (modal responses in bold) %	Agree (score 2)	Disagree (score 0)	Not sure/no answer (score 1)	Mean (SD)
MLD is very low attainment across the curriculum subjects	**18** **53%**	4 12%	12 36%	1.41 (0.70)
MLD is very low attainment across the curriculum subjects *and* very low intellectual abilities	**15** **44%**	5 15%	14 41%	1.29 (.72)
MLD involves learning difficulties that are *not* specific learning difficulties NOR severe intellectual disabilities	**19** **56%**	1 3%	14 41%	1.53 (0.56)
The difficulties identified as MLD are not easily differentiated from low attainment	**19** **56%**	1 3%	14 41%	1.53 (0.56)
The difficulties identified as MLD arise mainly from social and familial disadvantage	4 12%	11 32%	**19** **56%**	0.79 (.64)
The difficulties identified as MLD should not be regarded as an intellectual disability	12 35%	3 9%	**19** **56%**	1.26 (0.62)
The concept of MLD is problematic and is better not be used	4 12%	13 38%	**17** **50%**	0.73 (0.67)

The teaching approaches questionnaire set out to examine what pedagogic/teaching strategies teachers developed for pupils with MLD after using Lesson Study in their classes. The questionnaire responses were grouped into ten separate categories as shown in Figure 6.4, where the number in brackets represents the number of times this type of approach was mentioned by teachers. It can be seen that the approaches that teachers reported using were varied and covered many different areas including specific approaches such as using visual aids, memory-enhancing techniques, motivation of the students as well as more 'traditional' approaches like using differentiated materials. Of the ten categories, the three most commonly used were differentiation, multi-modal/sensory approaches and grouping and peer relationships/support (see Ylonen and Norwich, 2012 for a more detailed discussion). In general, differentiation was interpreted by teachers in a broader sense and not just as a way to provide different tasks for different students. Hence, such areas as providing variety of resources for pupils with different learning styles, using different types of questioning and providing specific individual support were mentioned. Figure 6.5 shows a model of teaching approaches, which was developed from the findings about the teaching approaches by re-analysing, merging and simplifying the existing themes. The model illustrates that the teachers were not using a specialist MLD pedagogy (as discussed in Chapter 3), but instead were making use of generic teaching strategies that they extended and/or intensified in different ways for teaching pupils with MLD.

To conclude, the findings about teachers' attitudes and beliefs demonstrate complexity and inconsistencies regarding their views on special educational needs and MLD. Although a higher percentage of the teachers believed that MLD is about low attainment only rather than low attainment and low

1 Differentiation (55) e.g. same general task at different levels; different materials
2 Multi-modal/sensory approaches (55) e.g. regular use of film and music; ICT
3 Grouping and peer relationships/support (50) e.g. use group activities; varied methods of allocation
4 Assessment of learning (41) e.g. checking understanding during lessons and checking outcomes at end of lessons; success criteria checklists
5 Motivational approaches (31), e.g. praise and positive encouragement; making tasks achievable
6 Working with additional adults (19) e.g. TAs deployed to support pupils
7 Adult-pupil communication (18) e.g. different kinds of questioning; encouraging discussion
8 Memory and consolidation (16) e.g. use visuals to enhance memory; repetition to support memory; building on previous lesson/learning
9 Activity based learning (13) e.g. role play
10 Pedagogic methods / assumptions (8) e.g. scaffolding and one-to-one coaching

Figure 6.4 *Pedagogic approaches referred to in questionnaire*

1 Broad pedagogic approach:
   (a) Learner centredness
   (b) Activity based learning
   (c) Assessment for learning
2 Varied input (multi-modal/sensory approaches)
3 Adapt cognitive demand:
   (a) Level/style (differentiation)
   (b) Memory/consolidation
4 Motivational approaches
5 Learning relationships:
   (a) Grouping and peer support
   (b) Adult–pupil communication
6 Working with additional adults

Figure 6.5 *A model of pedagogic approaches relevant to teaching pupils with MLD*

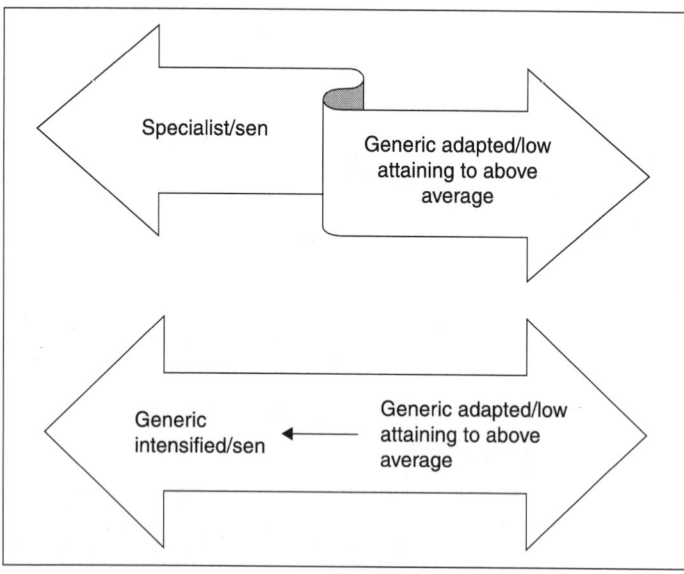

Figure 6.6 *Two models of pedagogy relevant to teaching pupils with MLD*

cognitive abilities, most disagreed or were not sure that MLD was a problematic concept that should not be used. This can be seen to reflect prevailing uncertainties about what moderate learning difficulties are and how the needs of these pupils should be catered for in both theory and in practice.

The teaching approaches used and developed by the teachers in the project reflect a broad and multifaceted concept of pedagogy relevant to pupils identified as having MLD. This included some well-known generic pedagogic approaches, adaptations to cognitive demand, varied input modes and the importance of motivational and learning relationships (see Figure 6.5). It was seen that teaching relevant to pupils with MLD was not just about cognitive demand or about simple ideas of differentiation. Most importantly, the analysis indicated that there were no distinct or specific pedagogic approaches for pupils identified as having MLD that were not also relevant to others without MLD (e.g. low attainment or other SEN). The teachers were not using a specific MLD pedagogy, but were making use of generic teaching strategies that they had selected and further developed and adapted through the Lesson Study process. These strategies have been extended and/or intensified in different ways for teaching pupils with MLD, as depicted in the second model in Figure 6.6. The findings are consistent with a model of pedagogy that assumes that teaching approaches are extensions and intensifications of general pedagogic approaches (Fletcher-Campbell, 2004) and consistent with the concept of a 'continuum of pedagogic strategies' as a position about the specialization of teaching for pupils with SEN (Norwich and Lewis, 2005).

The Lesson Study process: contexts, mechanisms and outcomes

Realist evaluation aims to field test a programme theory, which consists of statements about how specific mechanisms (M) in certain contexts (C) result in programme outcomes (O); represented as C-M-O links. This programme theory is then refined in response to various data sources. The aim of this research strand was to examine empirically how Lesson Study outcomes arise from specific processes in particular contexts (see above for a broader discussion about Lesson Study research). Using previous Lesson Study and school improvement research literature and in consultation with Lesson Study specialists a programme theory of Lesson Study of C-M-Os was designed for school and teacher-level processes. Some broad areas that were covered in the process theory included, for example, senior leader support, school's CPD practices, Lesson Study team meetings and collaboration, MLD teaching approaches, development of practical and pedagogic knowledge, and teacher confidence.

Based on the theory of teacher and school level C-M-Os, 66 statements were formulated for a survey questionnaire (see Appendix B). These were rated using a four-point scale (definitely not; slightly; mostly; definitely; with a 'can't say' option). After piloting and revising the questionnaire it was sent to 28 participating teachers at the end of the phase 1 using an online survey tool (Survey-Monkey). Responses were received from 16 teachers from 11 different schools.

The interview schedule was designed based on the Lesson Study process theory and it had six broad areas covering the C-M-Os at both teacher and school levels. Interviewing from this methodological perspective involved asking questions relevant to these six areas in order to learn about the informants' 'theories' about Lesson Study. As Pawson and Tilley (1997: 218) have suggested: 'the research act . . . involves "learning" the stakeholder's theories, formalizing them, "teaching" them back to the informant, who then is in a position to comment upon, clarify and further refine the key ideas'. Nine interviews were carried out with a sample of participating teachers from Lesson Study teams in five schools between May and July 2011. The teachers were chosen to represent schools that had different experiences of the Lesson Study process. Eight of the teachers were female and one was male; three were aged 20–30, two aged 31–40, and four aged 41–50.

The analysis presented below focuses on highlighting some of the main findings of the process survey and interviews (see Ylonen and Norwich, 2013 for the full discussion of the findings).

Table 6.5 shows the four highest-rated teacher-level context, mechanism and outcome statements. It can be seen that regarding the Lesson Study context the teachers felt prepared for Lesson Study as well as supported by the University team and web resources developed for the project, but had some ambivalence about support for Lesson Study by senior teachers. However, a majority of the teachers agreed ('mostly' and 'definitely' rating ranges), that senior leaders supported the project. The highest-rated teacher outcomes were about increased confidence in trying out novel teaching approaches, more willingness to change teaching, improved quality of planning and increased capability to plan and differentiate in teaching pupils with MLD.

Table 6.6 outlines the four highest-rated school-level context, mechanism and outcome statements. This shows that these schools were rated as committed to professional development, inclusion and innovation. The two most highly rated school mechanisms, both in the 'mostly' to 'definitely' range, were about senior teachers valuing professional development and encouraging involvement in collaborative professional development. There was less agreement about the school supporting its commitment to Lesson Study as shown by a lower mean rating about timetable flexibility for Lesson Study meetings. All the school-level mean outcome ratings were in the 'slightly' to 'mostly' range, indicating some issues about holding regular meetings, feeling supported in Lesson Study and other teachers showing interest in Lesson Study.

Table 6.5 Teacher-level ratings for contexts, mechanisms and outcomes

Teacher contexts	N	Mean	SD	Descriptor range
There is a high level of preparation and support for the project by the university team	16	3.63	0.62	Mostly–definitely
Teachers are committed to the project despite a degree of indifference by senior leaders/department	16	3.44	0.51	Mostly–definitely
Teachers feel supported by senior leaders in the project	14	3.36	0.63	Mostly–definitely
The web resources are of high quality	13	3.15	0.69	Mostly–definitely
Teacher mechanisms				
Teachers feel less threatened to scrutinize their own teaching	16	3.88	0.34	Mostly–definitely
The LS process increases teachers' interest in SEN in subject teaching	16	3.88	0.34	Mostly–definitely
The LS process increases teachers' interest in lesson development for pupils with MLD	16	3.81	0.40	Mostly–definitely
The LS process enhances teachers' confidence in teaching pupils with MLD	15	3.73	0.46	Mostly–definitely
Teacher outcomes				
More confidence to try out novel teaching approaches in lessons	16	3.81	0.40	Mostly–definitely
More willingness to make changes to usual teaching approaches	15	3.67	0.62	Mostly–definitely
The LS process has improved quality of planning of teaching	16	3.44	0.63	Mostly–definitely
Increased capability to plan and differentiate in teaching pupils with MLD	16	3.44	0.73	Mostly–definitely

Ratings from 1–4.

When interviewed the teachers reported very different views about the various contexts that either supported or hindered the Lesson Study process. The level of support given by senior leaders to the Lesson Study project varied widely in the schools from being very strong through neutral to being weak. Some teachers reported, for example, that:

They [senior teachers] have not been obstructive, but neither constructive. They love it when you [the teachers] do these things because it looks good on paper and it's good for the school, but they don't want to know more and leave you to get on with it. They gave permission for the project and were grateful for the money, but that's it.

Table 6.6 School-level ratings for contexts, mechanisms and outcomes

School contexts	N	Mean	SD	Descriptor range
School is actively committed to inclusion	16	3.75	0.68	Mostly–definitely
School is used to getting outside advice and support for development work	14	3.6	0.65	Mostly–definitely
Schools is actively committed to CPD	16	3.50	0.89	Mostly–definitely
School has a history of innovative developments	15	3.33	0.72	Mostly–definitely
School mechanisms				
Senior teachers see the importance of CPD	14	3.64	0.63	Mostly–definitely
School encourages teachers to participate in collaborative CPD	16	3.37	0.89	Mostly–definitely
School supports its commitment to the project	15	3.00	0.82	Mostly–definitely
Timetable flexibilities enable teachers to meet regularly	15	2.73	1.22	Slightly–mostly
School outcomes				
Attendance at meetings is regular and prioritised	16	2.88	1.15	Slightly–mostly
LS teachers feel supported by senior leaders in their LS work	15	2.80	1.08	Slightly-mostly
Senior teachers and those with SEN and CPD responsibilities encourage LS teachers	15	2.67	1.23	Slightly–mostly
Some teachers who are not in the LS team want to join in or get involved	15	2.40	1.12	Slightly–mostly

Ratings from 1–4.

Many of the teachers who were interviewed highlighted that they had used much of their own free time to undertake the Lesson Study project, but had different attitudes to this. Some teachers suggested that they had not requested much time away from their usual class teaching, because they had been able to carry out the Lesson Study work around their other commitments at the school. Some highlighted that their personal enthusiasm for the project and willingness to work outside school hours – normally after school – had been fundamental for the success of the project. Despite being able to arrange for cover to release them for the project (schools received funding for this), some of the teachers did not want to opt for this unless absolutely necessary. As one of the teachers pointed out, they did not want other areas of their teaching practice to suffer. However, one teacher pointed out that she had to come to the school even during her days off to work on the project, explaining that if she had been 'unwilling to do this, the whole project may not have worked out'.

In terms of outcomes of the Lesson Study process, there were more specific positive outcomes referred to in interviews that were not covered in the Lesson Study process questionnaire discussed above. These were about the enhanced capability to lesson plan, to deploy specific kinds of previously unused pedagogic strategies and to become aware of pedagogic knowledge relevant to teaching pupils with MLD and about teaching generally. Research by authors such as Puchner and Taylor (2006), Sims and Walsh (2009) and Rock and Wilson (2005) has alluded to similar Lesson Study outcomes in other countries. The following quotes from the teachers interviewed demonstrate these types of outcomes:

> As planning has been meticulous for Lesson Study, it shows what impact this can have on lessons . . . extra planning pays off as the lessons are better as a result, even for an experienced teacher . . . looking at the specific needs of students means that you are more aware of the needs of all students.
>
> It was interesting to see how students respond to different things. Initial assumptions were often wrong.
>
> Teachers often start with assessment criteria and work backwards and this does not allow things to be found out about wider learning.

Discussion

The questionnaire analysis pointed to the significance of the collaborative and constructive aspects of Lesson Study process and its capacity to make teachers more aware of their implicit practitioner knowledge (see Ylonen and Norwich, 2013 for a more in-depth discussion). The interviews underlined how the above positive outcomes were linked to two main processes, team observation of the research lessons and to risk-taking, both of which were consistent with the questionnaire findings. The observation process, which is an integral element of the Lesson Study method, emerged as a key strategy for the teachers to become more attuned to the way their students respond to specific pedagogical approaches. From this we can suggest that the Lesson Study team observation enabled direct formative assessment of teaching in the research lessons that then informed the subsequent planning of the next research lesson. The risk-taking when planning lesson can be seen to be supported by other aspects of the process: teamwork, good working relationships and a no-blame and less threatening environment; these were referred to in the interviews and questionnaire findings. These findings are consistent with the conclusions about the benefits to be gained from risk-taking in teaching in other Lesson Study research (see e.g. Lieberman, 2009; Dudley, 2012; Yoshida, 2012). Overall, this study also provides evidence that confirms the conjecture of Lewis *et al.* (2006), made on the basis of extensive US Lesson Study work, that Lesson Study strengthens three pathways to teaching improvement: first, teachers' knowledge, second, teachers' commitment and community, and third, learning resources.

This study also confirms findings from other research about Lesson Study (e.g. Rock and Wilson, 2005; Lee, 2008; Perry and Lewis, 2009; Lim *et al.*, 2011) about the contextual factors that are important for this method to be used effectively.[1] Our analyses showed issues in some schools over timetabling Lesson Study meetings and the support of senior teachers. The interview data showed this is more depth, while also showing that some teachers had to put in extra time beyond their usual work time and that in some schools, despite the funding for their release from regular teaching, the funds were not used as expected. So, where contextual factors were supportive, teachers experienced Lesson Study as leading to positive outcomes. In other schools the timetable and management did not enable Lesson Study to operate optimally.

The interview analysis provided some check on the validity of the Lesson Study programme theory, which was used to design the questionnaire statements. This showed that some of the process (mechanism) statements could have been formulated more in terms of the details of the Lesson Study processes, for example observation, and less on processes linked to outcomes, for example, processes linked to enhanced teacher confidence in teaching. These findings were used to revise and refine the initial programme theory for future use.

Pupil outcomes following Lesson Study in phase 2 of the project

Pupil outcomes in phase 1 were only monitored through qualitative summative accounts provided in the Lesson Study case reports. Though many positive pupil outcomes were reported, these were mainly focused on changes in learning behaviours and motivation and only in fairly general terms. Although there were a few specific positive reports about academic/cognitive learning gains, these did not feature in teacher's own evaluation of pupil outcomes. Subsequently, it was decided to introduce a more focused way of setting learning goals for case pupils in the phase 2 design of the Lesson Study procedure. Not only would this help the Lesson Study teachers plan their research lessons in terms of more focused learning goals, but this would also provide a way of monitoring pupil learning and outcomes for phase 2. This was to be done by a method known as Goal Monitoring and Evaluation (GME) – a systematic goal setting and monitoring system (Jones *et al.*, 2006; Dunsmuir *et al.*, 2009). The GME method has been used fairly widely to evaluate the outcomes of many kinds of programmes as well as service contexts, initially under the name Goal Attainment Scaling (GAS) (Jones *et al.*, 2006). Previous evaluation (Dunsmuir *et al.*, 2009) indicates that it is best used when it meets these criteria:

1. there is advance specification of the expected goal
2. at least three goals are used
3. there is independent review/assessment of levels attained

In the version of GME used in phase 2 the Lesson Study teams were asked to set up three goals per case pupil before the Lesson Study cycle commenced. In addition, the teams were asked to specify three levels on an 11-point progression line for each of the case pupil's goals (ordinal scale). These levels were referenced in terms of these goals: two before the programme started (a baseline level and an expected level), and one after the programme (an achieved level). In this way, the participating teachers in Lesson Study were required to assess pupils' achieved levels by comparison with prior baseline and expected levels. They were asked to give their own descriptor for all three levels and evidence for that descriptor (see Appendix C for an example of a completed GME template). The Lesson Study team were expected to set levels so that there was some moderation of the attained levels. The attained levels at the end of the Lesson Study cycle were then used to evaluate pupil outcomes in terms of any progress relative to baseline and expected level (progress as expected; more than expected, less than expected or no progress). The degree of goal attainment could also be analysed in terms of the kinds of goals set in the lesson studies.

Completed GME data were received from 9 of the 15 schools (several Lesson Study teams gave incomplete data while a few gave no data). This comprised data from 21 separate Lesson Studies with 1–2 case pupils per Lesson Study. In total, teachers set 69 pupil goals in these lesson studies. Table 6.7 shows that out of these 69 Lesson Study goals, progress was met or exceeded in just over half of the goals (54 per cent; 37 goals) as assessed by the Lesson Study teachers. Out of these 37 goals, progress was as expected in 25 per cent of goals (17) and more than expected in 29 per cent (20) of goals. In just under half of the goals pupils' made some progress, but did not meet the expected level (46 per cent or 32 goals). This shows that there were no goals for which the case pupils did not make *some* progress from the baseline level.

Personal goals for pupils with MLD were analysed in terms of whether they were curriculum subject-related, e.g. 'developing written ideas independently' or 'demonstrating understanding of auditory and visual information', or referred to a learning process, e.g. 'being less disruptive and argumentative' or 'having more confidence in group activities'. Some goals were both subject-related and about learning process, e.g. 'independently offering contributions to class discussions and begin to record ideas in a more independent way' or 'being more frequently engaged in activities when emphasis is on using key vocabulary' (see Table 6.8). Overall, 49 of the 69 goals or 71 per cent were about learning process only, while the remaining 20 goals or 29 per cent were goals that were subject-related or subject-related linked to learning process. Table 6.8 also shows the level of attainment (scored 0–3 as shown in the table) by these three different kinds of goals. This indicates little difference between the mean goal attainment scores for learning process

Table 6.7 Goal monitoring and evaluation: 15 schools, 21 Lesson Studies, 69 goals set

Progress	Percentages
Progress as expected	25 (n = 17)
Progress more than expected	29 (n = 20)
Progress but not met the expected level	46 (n = 32)
No progress	0 (n = 0)
Total	**100%**

Table 6.8 Level of goal attainment by kind of goal

	None (score = 0)	<Expected (score = 1)	As expected (score = 2)	>Expected (score = 3)	Total	Mean score
Subject-related	0	6	5	3	14	1.79
Learning process + subject-related	0	2	2	2	6	2.00
Learning process	0	24	10	15	49	1.82
Total	0	32/46%	17/25%	20/29%	69	1.83

and subject-related goals (in the range 1.79–1.83). The mean score for the relatively few combined subject-related and learning process goals was slightly higher at 2.0.

To conclude, the goal-setting and monitoring made it possible for goal attainment to be examined for the individual case pupils following the Lesson Study cycle. Analysis showed that there was progress from the start to the end of the Lesson Study cycle for just under half of the pupils with MLD at expected or beyond the expected levels. The rest made progress but less than expected. It is worth pointing out that although there was a gap in the goal attainment data (completed by 60 per cent of the phase 2 schools), we know from analysis of the Lesson Study case reports that five of the teams out of the six where we had no GME data reported very specific positive pupil learning outcomes following the Lesson Study process. These are encouraging findings, and suggest that the Lesson Study process through teachers focusing on the learning goals of the case pupils resulted in improved outcomes for the pupils.

Ethnographic research findings: four case study school vignettes

Ethnographic research was undertaken in phase 2 of the project to gain a more thorough understanding about the Lesson Study process in a sample of the participating schools. Four schools were asked to take part in this strand of research, which consisted of observations of a number of research lessons and review/planning meetings as well as interviews with some of the participating teachers in these schools. In total, 13 research lessons and 13 review/planning meetings were observed and 6 interviews were undertaken between late 2011 and mid-2012.

In this section of the chapter, short vignettes of the four case study schools are outlined focusing on the main features of the Lesson Studies undertaken, the difficulties experienced by the teachers and the main outcomes of the Lesson Study process for the teachers and the schools. The aim is to provide a snapshot of the main 'lessons learned' from each of the four schools and bringing to light some of the differences between these four schools in terms of obstacles encountered and outcomes gained. The section ends with some general concluding thoughts drawing on all four case studies.

The four schools discussed above all had very different experiences of the Lesson Study process, encountered different types of obstacles and gained different outcomes. The common difficulty experienced to some extent by all the schools – with different effects – was the lack of time to undertake the

Table 6.9 Vignette 1: Riverside School

Background: Riverside School is a large secondary school (11–18-year-olds) with Academy status. The school specializes in mathematics and ICT/ computing.

Lesson Study 1 team (LS1): RE teacher; history teacher (+ assistant SENCO and deputy principal)

Lesson Study 2 team (LS2): history teacher; RE teacher (+ assistant SENCO and SENCO)

Senior management team (SMT) involvement: SMT gave permission for the project, but no further involvement. Deputy principal of the school was nominally part of LS1 team, but was not fully engaged in the process

LS1 and LS2 topic: Using LS to develop teaching approaches that help students with MLD to grow in confidence and self-esteem

Difficulties experienced: process time-consuming; lack of interest and support from SMT, feeling expressed by the LS teachers that deputy principal wanted to use LS for his own agenda (e.g. focusing on OFSTED criteria and high-achieving pupils) rather than the project agenda (pupils with MLD). The amount of extra work involved seen as overwhelming by one teacher (T2)

Main outcomes: T1 saw benefits in the process and developed knowledge and teaching approaches for pupils with MLD. Although T2 saw broadly similar benefits to T1 she remained sceptical about LS mainly because of its time-consuming nature and for cover reasons. There was no evidence of enjoyment in the process by either teacher. Both teachers are unlikely to continue using LS in the future and there was no impact of LS on the school more widely.

Table 6.10 Vignette 2: Heathview School

Background: Heathview School is an average-sized secondary school with Academy status (11–18-year-olds). The school specialises in science, mathematics and computing. The school has engaged in various initiatives in recent years.

LS1/LS2 team: two geography/humanities teachers; deputy principal (cum science teacher)

SMT involvement: SMT members initiated the project and fully supported the process with active involvement from deputy principal throughout the process in both LS1 and LS2

LS1 topic: Using LS to improve students' writing skills in order to fully complete tasks; engaging pupils in appropriate communications with peers

LS2 topic: Using LS to improve the writing skills of students' with MLD, to write appropriate and accurate sentences as well as enabling them to positively engage with work and tasks in humanities

Difficulties experienced: Meetings were scheduled at the start with cover arrangements made where needed – teachers were reluctant to take time off timetable as this was seen as disruptive and preferred to meet during lunchtime and/or after school, which both teachers were happy to do

Main outcomes: The LS team was cohesive and worked well together. All LS team members enjoyed the process and saw clear benefits of LS in improving teaching and learning. Collaborative aspects of planning were seen as beneficial – planning of teaching has improved; more knowledge about case pupils, and other pupils as a result of observing them closely; more confidence to try new teaching strategies for SEN pupils.

process. In some schools, like Heathview, this difficulty was acknowledged, but it was well-managed via effective timetabling of the research lessons and planning/review meetings. In other schools, like Riverside, the extra time required to undertake Lesson Study caused unexpected workload pressures, which were undesirable.

Another factor that related to the overall success of the Lesson Study process was senior leader support – or a lack of support – for the process. It is notable that in Heathview school in which the Lesson Study process evolved without major difficulties, the involvement and support of a senior teacher was strong throughout the process. It appears that the involvement of the deputy principal – his interest in Lesson Study, support for the process and insightful input in Lesson Study planning and review meetings – was fundamental for the success of the Lesson Study process in the school. It also meant that after the project ended, the team was asked to give presentations

Table 6.11 Vignette 3: Valley School

Background: Valley School is a smaller-than-average-secondary school (11–18-year-olds). The school specialises in science, mathematics and computing.

LS team: English teacher; art teacher; SENCO (in some parts of the process)

SMT involvement: SMT gave its support for the project, but was not otherwise involved

LS1 and LS2 topic: use LS to improve confidence, learning and comprehension of the pupils with MLD and to support their independent working

Difficulties experienced: Valley School joined the project later than other schools because the teachers were not informed about the invitation to join the project in time (they therefore missed the first introductory conference, but had a LS workshop/briefing from one of the consultants); time-consuming nature of LS

Main outcomes: both teachers found the collaborative aspects of planning and reviewing helpful; new teaching strategies and approaches were trialled and shared; more awareness about the case pupils and the way they react in class. It is possible that the school will use elements of the LS process in the future.

to wider school staff and senior leaders about the Lesson Study. There was an interest in continuing with Lesson Study in some form in the school because the outcomes were seen as beneficial. In the other three schools senior leader support for the Lesson Study process was lacking – and none of the participating teachers reported a clear desire to continue using Lesson Study in their schools after the project ended.

It is worth elaborating on two different experiences to illustrate some possible pitfalls in the implementation of Lesson Study. The first example from Valley School highlights the importance of collaborative planning, while the second example from Bishopsgate School highlights the prevailing misconceptions about Lesson Study by one of the participating teachers.

Although the two teachers at Valley School worked together well in the Lesson Study team, there was little evidence of real collaborative planning of the research lessons. It therefore appeared that the lessons in both Lesson Study1 and Lesson Study 2 were mostly individually planned, though jointly reviewed, and that Lesson Study was an 'add-on' to a normal lesson in terms of team observation and review meetings after the lessons. This perhaps represents a missed opportunity, as it is often through the collaborative planning that real gains are made in creating new knowledge and in gaining new insights in the Lesson Study process.

Table 6.12 Vignette 4: Bishopsgate School

Background: Bishopsgate School is an average-sized Church of England voluntary aided specialist science and sports college for 11–16-year-olds.

LS team: SEN specialist English teacher; English and drama teacher (and nominally one member of SMT)

SMT involvement: SMT member initiated the project, but was not fully involved in the process

LS1 topic: Developing teaching approaches for students with MLD to improve concentration, speaking and listening skills

LS2 topic: improving group work skills in the context of a series of drama lessons on the technical aspects of production

Difficulties experienced: process time-consuming; lack of interest from SMT and other teaching staff, small and isolated team, misunderstanding with teacher that LS would be a 'miracle wand' to improve teaching

Main outcomes: T1 saw clear benefits in the process and developed and trialled new teaching approaches for MLD which T1 will continue to use in the future; T1 enjoyed the collaborative aspects of planning and saw the LS process as valuable. LS did not fulfil T2's expectations, i.e. that LS would be a radically different and useful technique to improve teaching. T2 was sceptical about LS and its promises: LS does not seem to fit the English school context. T2 is unlikely to continue using LS in the future.

At Bishopsgate School one of the two teachers expressed very negative views about Lesson Study and its benefits. It appears that this teacher had misunderstood the purpose of Lesson Study. He did not see Lesson Study as a strategy with principles which, when used collaboratively in teams, can lead to insights about the teaching and learning process which in turn can result in better outcomes for both teachers and learners. Instead, this teacher based his views about Lesson Study on his own negative experiences without analysing them more fully: the teacher was disappointed in Lesson Study and concluded that it does not belong to the English school culture.

The four case study school vignettes have been used to demonstrate the range of different experiences that teachers and schools can have when engaged in the Lesson Study process; though not necessarily typical of all participating schools. These analyses also show that external and internal conditions – related to individuals, the Lesson Study teacher teams and the wider school cultures, for example – exist in schools, which have an important impact on the Lesson Study process and how Lesson Study evolves in schools. These conditions can either promote or hinder the development of successful Lesson Study outcomes for pupils, teachers and schools.

Conclusions

This chapter has discussed findings in the evaluation wing of the two-year Development and Research Lesson Study-MLD project. The aim of the concluding section is to integrate these findings and to discuss their wider significance to practice, for example to teachers, teaching and schools. The policy implications of this research, such as the current development and debates about SEN policy in England, will be discussed in Chapter 7.

The first wider aspect of the research discussed above was about the category of MLD: its identification in schools, teachers' beliefs about MLD and teaching approaches for MLD. One of the main findings was that many of the pupils who had been labelled as having MLD in these schools cannot be seen to belong to this category as conventionally defined and assessed by using standardized measures such as the British Ability Scales. It was seen that only those pupils who had a statement of SEN were close to being in the lowest second percentile in their reasoning and literacy scores for the age group. The research findings suggest that pupils who are low attaining in some areas of the curriculum, such as literacy, have come to be identified as having MLD but are not different from those who are below average in their attainment and not identified as having SEN.

The concept of MLD was found to be confusing to many teachers and they were commonly unsure about what role intellectual functioning plays in the identification of MLD. It was also seen that the pedagogic approaches used and developed by the participating teachers for teaching pupils with MLD were not specialist SEN teaching approaches, but general approaches that had been extended or intensified to use for pupils with MLD. These findings provide further evidence to show that the category of MLD is not well understood in theory, for example the official government definition of MLD, or in practice by schools and teachers. The fact that the project schools used widely different ways to identify MLD further illustrates this.

The second wider aspect of the research was about the Lesson Study process that was examined from different standpoints in the above sections. The realist evaluation that focused on the Lesson Study contexts, mechanisms and outcomes found that the teachers reported strongly positive outcomes of the process for themselves, while the outcomes for the schools were positive, but less so than they were at the teacher level. The findings indicated, for example, that by taking part in the Lesson Study process the teachers improved their planning of teaching, they had more confidence to try new approaches and they gained insights from Lesson Study observations and collaborative planning and reviewing of teaching, and had more awareness of the individual needs of pupils. In short, the teachers had gained more knowledge and awareness about the teaching and learning process.

It emerged that the context in which Lesson Study takes place in schools can support or hinder the Lesson Study process and is important for the overall success of the Lesson Study process. For example, the level of support and interest from senior leaders towards the Lesson Study work done by participating teachers emerged as important. In schools where participating teachers experienced this kind of support, the Lesson Study process evolved more smoothly. The ethnographic case studies illustrated the different experiences of the case study schools and revealed that in a school like Heathview, where senior leader support was strong (the Lesson Study team included a deputy principal), the overall outcomes were seen as highly positive by all team members. In schools such as Bishopsgate and Riverside a lack of genuine senior leader support made the process more difficult. Senior leader support was also related to another important factor in the case studies: time to undertake the Lesson Study process and willingness to establish a school timetable that enables professional learning, such as Lesson Study, to take place. In Heathview, although the team members acknowledged the fact that the Lesson Study process can be time-consuming, this was effectively managed from the outset with the support of the senior leaders in the school. However, some teachers in schools like Riverside were overwhelmed by the amount of time required to undertake the Lesson Study process, and this negatively impacted on their enjoyment of the process. The findings demonstrate the importance of the contextual factors for Lesson Study to become a sustained commitment in schools.

Improved learning outcomes of the case pupils (and other pupils in the Lesson Study classes) were widely reported by the teachers in this study. It was noted that all the case pupils (who were monitored) made gains in their learning outcomes as assessed by the teachers using a GME method. The findings indicate that the Lesson Study process enabled teachers to develop teaching approaches and a focus on the learning requirements of the pupils with MLD, who then showed gains in their learning. Although the findings about pupil outcomes cannot be simply generalized to other settings, they act as a clear demonstration of positive pupil learning outcomes in a particular context and use of Lesson Study. Our evidence of how improved pupil learning was linked to the Lesson Study process in the project schools is consistent with Lewis *et al.*'s (2009) assertion that improvements in teaching through Lesson Study leads to better student learning. Moreover, the findings show that a GME approach can be successfully used in efforts to create more robust evidence of pupil outcomes in Lesson Study contexts – an area where there are distinct gaps in research, knowledge and evidence.

It has been shown that the Lesson Study process offers potentially considerable benefits to pupils, teachers and schools – however, teachers and schools need to maintain a long-term commitment to Lesson Study in order to secure long-lasting outcomes. As this research shows, this can be challenging. It is also evident that Lesson Study evolves differently in every school. Teachers and schools engaged in Lesson Study will have different experiences of the process, will face different challenges along the way and will gain different benefits from the process. There is always an element of the unexpected when undertaking the Lesson Study process – the unexpected is perhaps one of the greatest opportunities that Lesson Study offers.

Appendix A: outline of the system of SEN in England (at the time of research; it is currently undergoing change)

Level of need	Nature of intervention
School Action	Additional to or different from the usual (differentiated) curriculum of the school. External agencies not involved. Recorded without categories in annual census.
School Action Plus	External support services are involved when the child does not make expected progress despite school interventions. Recorded with specification of categories in census.
Statement	A local authority, after undertaking statutory assessment, despite interventions at previous levels, issues a Statement (or record) of special educational needs and provision. Provision may be in ordinary or special schools. Recorded with specification of categories in census.

Source: DfES (2001).

Appendix B: teacher and school level statements (contexts, mechanisms and outcomes)

Teacher-level contexts

1. The Lesson Study teachers meet regularly with enough time to undertake Lesson Study process.
2. The Lesson Study teachers feel supported by senior teachers in the project.

3 Senior teachers support the Lesson Study teachers to find out about assessment and teaching approaches for use in Lesson Study.

4 Senior teachers support the Lesson Study work by enquiring about progress.

5 Teachers with SEN and CPD responsibilities support the Lesson Study work by enquiring about progress.

6 The Lesson Study teachers publicize project outcomes and outputs in the school with senior teacher support.

7 Individual teachers are committed to project goals and methods, despite some degree of senior and department indifference.

8 There is a high level of preparation and support for the project by the university team.

9 The web resources are of high quality.

Teacher-level mechanisms

1 The Project Conferences made you interested in teaching related CPD and its relevance to teaching pupils with MLD.

2 The Project Conferences enabled you to develop knowledge about teaching related CPD with relevance to teaching pupils with MLD.

3 The Lesson Study process makes you interested about special educational needs in your subject teaching.

4 The novelty and the practical relevance of the Lesson Study approach makes you interested in lesson development for teaching pupils with MLD.

5 Your wider awareness of the Lesson Study process enhances your confidence in teaching pupils with MLD.

6 The Lesson Study teaching group provides collaborative opportunities for you to share knowledge and skills with colleagues.

7 The Lesson Study teaching group provides a sharing of risk in innovating about teaching and more willingness to learn from errors.

8 Solidarity between teachers affirms your capabilities to innovate about lesson teaching.

9 The Lesson Study process provides dedicated time to reflect, plan and problem-solve in a supportive public setting.

10 Participating teachers use concepts and procedures associated with thinking skills and assessment for learning in their Lesson Study work.

11 Participating teachers in the Lesson Study process provide honest and constructive observations of research lessons to each other.

12 Participating teachers in the Lesson Study process carry out the procedures in an informed, thoughtful and adaptable way.

13 New ideas about MLDs and how to teach pupils with MLD are being created through the Lesson Study process.

14 The Lesson Study process provides a micro-focus on the learning of 1–2 students to enable a greater depth of analysis.

15 The Lesson Study process enables participating teachers to think of themselves operating in research mode about their teaching.

16 The Lesson Study process enables participating teachers to think about themselves as innovators in their schools.

17 The Lesson Study process focuses on learning outcomes and so builds teacher confidence to attain more challenging objectives.

18 Participating teachers feel less threatened to scrutinize their own teaching by focusing on pupil learning rather than evaluating teaching.

19 Participating teachers become more aware of their implicit teaching knowledge (practitioner knowledge)through the Lesson Study process.

Teacher-level outcomes

1 You have more theoretical and practical knowledge about Lesson Study (e.g. principles, methods and practical know-how for going about it).

2 You have deeper knowledge about your curriculum subject and subject pedagogy for pupils identified as having MLD.

3 You have more understanding about the nature and complexity of the learning needs of pupils with MLD.

4 You have more knowledge about how to overcome barriers to learning for pupils with MLD.

5 You have an increased capability to plan and differentiate in your teaching of pupils with MLD.

6 You have increased capability to engage pupils with MLD in their learning.

7 You have a more positive attitude to pupils identified as having MLD and to their inclusion in school and teaching.

8 You have more confidence to try out novel teaching approaches in lessons.

9 You have an increased ability to articulate aspects of practice.

10 You have more personal interest in providing quality teaching to all in your lesson planning and lessons.

11 You are more open to learning from others and exposing your teaching to others in safe settings.

12 You are more able and willing to examine your teaching to become aware of false assumptions and new possibilities.

13 You have more willingness to make changes to your usual teaching approaches.

14 You are more positive towards a dynamic concept of teaching as involving constant learning about how to deal with novel situations.

15 The Lesson Study process has improved the quality of planning of your teaching (and not just how to refine specific lesson plans).

School-level contexts

1 This school has a clear commitment to inclusion as a key value.

2 This school has an active commitment to Continuous Professional Development (CPD) as a long-term development strategy.

3 This school has a history of innovative developments relevant to its vision and values.

4 This school has some successful experiences of CPD about the development of teaching.

5 This school has some history of effective teacher collaboration projects and practices.

6 This school is used to getting outside advice and support for development work.

School-level mechanisms

1 Senior teachers with management responsibilities use opportunities to improve inclusive provision in the school.

2 Senior teachers with management responsibilities see the significance of CPD for inclusive provision.

3 Teachers with CPD responsibilities use opportunities to introduce CPD that supports teaching and learning.

4 Senior teachers are aware of the principles of Lesson Study as a CPD approach relevant to SEN/MLD.

5 The school actively supports its commitment to participate in the Lesson Study project.

6 Senior teachers appreciate the importance of CPD about teaching.

7 The school appreciates that CPD is for a longer-term development of teaching and not only for immediate school development planning.

8 The school encourages teachers to participate in collaborative CPD.

9 The school uses project funding creatively to enable teacher release to engage in the Lesson Study activities.

10 The school supplements outside CPD funding with its own resources.

11 Timetable flexibilities enable the Lesson Study teachers to meet regularly.

12 Support visits and contacts from the university team support participating teachers and others in their developmental work.

13 Support visits and contacts from the university team provide knowledge about Lesson Study methods relevant to teaching pupils with MLD.

School-level outcomes

1 The attendance at Lesson Study meetings is regular and given a high priority.

2 The Lesson Study teachers feel supported by senior leaders in the Lesson Study work.

3 Senior teachers and those with SEN and CPD responsibilities encourage the Lesson Study teachers.

4 Some teachers who are not in the Lesson Study team want to join or become involved.

Appendix C: example of a GME template filled in by a LS team

GOAL 1									
Be more frequently engaged in group activities when emphasis is on using key vocabulary									
Rating scale:									
	Low → High								
Baseline		X							
Expected						X			
Achieved						X			

Baseline descriptor	Is often disengaged in group activities when she needs to use vocabulary
Specific evidence for descriptor	Because of problems in written and verbal language tends to be disengaged and not participate
Expected descriptor	More frequent engagement in group activities
Specific evidence for descriptor	Increased participation, improved speech, increased confidence
Achieved descriptor	More frequent engagement in group activities
Specific evidence for descriptor	Participated more during question and answer sessions; vocabulary still limited but conversations contain more basic structure; more willing to write and less anxious about her work

Note

1 Correlational analysis of the process questionnaire data across 11 of the schools suggested that more supportive Lesson Study contexts tended to lead to more positive outcomes at school and teacher levels, as discussed in Ylonen and Norwich (2013).

7

What Have we Learned?

What are the Future Prospects and Ways Forward?

Brahm Norwich and Jeff Jones

Introduction

In this book, we have examined how the principles of Lesson Study work in practice for children and young people with learning difficulties. The book has covered theoretical, practical and research aspects of this collaborative developmental strategy. Although the main source of ideas and practices come from the Lesson Study-MLD project that was about secondary teaching, we have also included examples of Lesson Study in primary schools that have focused on pupils with learning difficulties.

One of the key features of Lesson Study is its collaborative professional learning and development nature; the bringing together of teachers with different knowledge and skills with a focus on intensive lesson-planning and review. In the Lesson Study-MLD project, this involved the interaction between class teachers from different subjects with teachers with a specialization in SEN, such as the SEN coordinators. What can arise from this collaboration is a mutual learning, innovativeness and enthusiasm that can prompt improvements in lesson planning and teaching that leads to enhanced pupil learning.

This collaboration between people with different knowledge and backgrounds was also found in the Lesson Study-MLD project team, the authors of this book. This book reflects a similar collaboration of colleagues from different areas of education, specialist backgrounds and roles. As the secondary school Lesson Study teams learned when they undertook several Lesson Study cycles, so the project team learned through two project phases how to integrate Lesson Study principles and procedures into the field of teaching pupils identified as having MLD. Members of the project team have background experiences and specialist knowledge covering professional learning and development, school improvement, advisory teaching, special needs-inclusive education and educational psychology. What has been learned from the project arises from this collaborative interchange. As a summary of some of the practices developed and key findings from the project, this book also represents a similar collaborative effort of the project team.

We have aimed to show how Lesson Study can promote developments in class teaching in an area that continues to challenge teachers, the teaching of pupils with learning difficulties. We have used the term learning difficulties to represent the range of difficulties in learning that covers the spectrum from MLD to low attainment, crossing the boundary between what is regarded as SEN and not SEN at a time when this boundary itself is about to change. We have also presented practical case examples of lesson studies across different curriculum subjects at primary and secondary schools.

Instead of summarizing the key points from each chapter in this final chapter, we have identified a range of keys themes as chapter sections to organize our discussion, conclusions and recommendations. The first theme will highlight the key features of the Lesson Study-MLD project, how it came to be initiated, undertaken and evaluated in a changing policy context. The second theme is about the category of MLD and its significance for teaching pupils identified as having MLD. The next two themes are about Lesson Study and what has been learned from the project about what counts as a quality Lesson Study and the organizational and leadership conditions necessary to enable quality Lesson Studies. The final section of the chapter discusses future prospects and recommendations for the extension of Lesson Study to other areas of teaching children with SEN beyond MLD, as well as ways in which Lesson Study can be adapted and embedded for wider educational purposes.

MLD category: its usefulness and significance for teaching pupils identified as having MLD

Ruth Gwernan-Jones outlined in Chapter 3 some of the complexities and uncertainties about the MLD category in its use in the UK since its introduction following the Warnock Report (DES, 1978). The key problem lies with its definition and how this is put into operation in practice in the education system. Although this is a specific UK category, the issues are historical and international. The terms used and boundaries between different forms of learning difficulties and disabilities reflect questions about the purposes of special educational and disability categories in this field. One of the key issues in the UK is whether MLD is very low educational attainment across the curriculum or whether it is low attainment and low intellectual functioning (problems in 'understanding concepts'). However, this dilemma tends to be less of a problem in other countries where there has been less concern about the use of IQ or general cognitive ability tests and where identifying intellectual disability is based on such tests (in Chapter 6 and Norwich *et al.*, 2012).

Though the main aim of the Lesson Study-MLD project was to apply Lesson Study to improve teaching and learning, the project provided a unique opportunity to study how the MLD category was used in the project secondary schools. This has been an unexplored question, reflecting the relative lack of research in the MLD field in the UK. So, the project research findings, reported in Chapter 6, are notable. Many of the pupils in phase 1 project schools who were identified as having MLD cannot be seen to belong to this category when it is defined by very low levels of reasoning ('problems with concepts') and literacy levels (at or below the second percentile). Only those pupils identified as having MLD who also had a Statement of SEN, were close to the second percentile in their reasoning and literacy scores, the conventional cut-off level. These research findings indicate that some pupils in these schools who are low attaining in some areas of the curriculum, such as literacy, have come to be identified as having MLD, but are not different from those who are below average in their attainment and not identified as having SEN.

The concept of MLD was found to be confusing to many teachers and there were different views and uncertainty about what role intellectual functioning plays in the identification of MLD (see Chapter 6 and Ylonen and Norwich, 2012). These findings provide further evidence to show that the category of MLD is not well understood in theory, for example the current official government definition of MLD, or in practice by schools and teachers. As discussed in Chapter 3, MLD is an area and category of SEN that has been much neglected in educational research and development in the UK, despite the relatively high proportion of pupils identified under this category. The relatively high UK incidence compares with a much lower incidence of mild mental retardation, the US counterpart to MLD (McMillan *et al.*, 1996). Mild mental retardation, which is now called mild intellectual disabilities, made up 8.6 per cent of all pupils identified as having disabilities in education in the USA in 2007 (US IDEA statistics: this covers mild, moderate and severe intellectual disabilities with mild being the largest subgroup; this compares with about 23 per cent in England). This is partly to do with the tighter US definition in terms of both intellectual functioning below 70 on a standard scale (IQ scale) and low adaptive functioning outside school. The lower US incidence is also associated with more children being identified as having specific learning disabilities, the counterpart to specific learning difficulties (SpLD) in the UK.

In the USA, MacMillan *et al.* (1996) questioned the basis for a reliable and distinct category of mild mental retardation (mild intellectual disability) in terms that are relevant to the use of MLD in the UK. They recommend that intellectual disabilities be reserved for more severe forms of difficulties, and that a more descriptive term be used for those currently identified as having mild intellectual disabilities. In the UK, there is the equivalent issue of whether pupils identified as having MLD are to be considered as at the lowest end of the continuum of lower attaining pupils, or whether they have a mild–moderate intellectual disability. This is the fundamental issue raised by the research arising from the Lesson Study-MLD project. What are the boundaries of SEN and how do we define SEN – what counts as a disability in education? The rationale for using a learner category, like MLD, is usually justified in terms of:

1. whether there are distinctive characteristics associated with the category;
2. whether the category provides a basis for communication and understanding of particular difficulties;
3. whether the category has significance and is useful for teaching;
4. providing the grounds for allocating additional resources; and
5. providing a basis for a positive social identity and solidarity of those who have the difficulty (Norwich, 2013b).

Research from the project questions whether there are distinctive characteristics associated with the MLD category. Other research from the project also raises questions about whether the MLD category has significance and is useful for teaching. As explained in Chapter 6, the pedagogic approaches that were used and developed during Lesson Studies by the participating teachers for pupils with MLD were not specialist or distinctive SEN teaching approaches. General pedagogic approaches were used and developed, e.g. task differentiation, multi-sensory approaches, learner grouping and memory supports and consolidation. These were extended or intensified through Lesson Study for use with pupils identified as having MLD in their subject teaching. These findings are further evidence for the ideas discussed in Chapter 3 that teaching pupils with MLD is more in keeping with the *unique differences* than a *general differences* position about pedagogy. In the unique differences position teaching pupils with learning difficulties involves differences in pedagogic strategies, but these differ by degree (a continuum of pedagogic strategies) not by kind (as in the general differences position).

As also discussed in Chapter 3, the use of teaching informed by ideas about working memory and thinking/intellectual skills (cognitive modifiability) is relevant to teaching pupils with learning difficulties. However, as argued there and shown in the Lesson Study-MLD findings, these approaches are not specific to those identified as having MLD (as they have been shown to be relevant to pupils identified with other SEN/disabilities). These approaches are also relevant to pupils who have difficulties in learning but whose SEN status is uncertain. This point is illustrated well by combining the two key findings of the project research; (1) the spread of the MLD category to pupils with below-average attainments (the uncertainty about MLD/SEN boundary) and (2) the continuum of pedagogic strategies revealed in analysing the teaching used and developed in the Lesson Studies.

Another way of considering the significance of the MLD category for teaching pupils identified as having MLD is to analyse the different kinds of knowledge used by teachers in their Lesson Studies. There is evidence from the case studies in Chapters 4 and 5, the survey research in Chapter 6 and ongoing analysis of project data that teachers drew on their own professional knowledge about general teaching approaches in designing their research lessons and then reviewed and developed these approaches. However, some teachers also followed the Lesson Study model that was introduced to them by drawing on research and literature-based knowledge about teaching approaches, e.g. about group work in lessons. This is not specific to MLD or learning difficulties but relates to more personalized and participative learning approaches. There were also some teachers who drew on approaches that have been more closely associated with MLD, about working memory and cognitive modifiability (thinking and intellectual strategies).

There were two Lesson Studies conducted in phase 1 of the project, which illustrate how Lesson Study can work in relation to teaching pupils with identified MLD that takes account of memory support. The first was the Lesson Study described as Case study 4 in Chapter 5, the second was an art lesson at another school (not reported as a case study). In the first Lesson Study, the teachers explicitly used working memory ideas in planning their history research lessons (drawing on Gathercole and Alloway's (2008) applications of working memory as a source; see Case study 4 in Chapter 5). This is an example of the explicit use of research-informed knowledge in their Lesson Study. In the art Lesson Study, the teachers aimed to find a way of supporting a pupil with MLD to draw a gargoyle. Through a process of trial and error, they came up with a way of presenting visual images of the parts of the gargoyle to support the visual memory of this pupil in the drawing process. This analysis of the drawing task, and the use of memory support, proved to be successful in enabling this pupil to enhance her drawing skills. This is an example of how Lesson Study can provide a framework for teachers to apply or develop theories of working memory into ideas for teaching. These cases illustrate the potential of Lesson Study to enable both the bottom-up and top-down development and use of relevant knowledge to enhance teaching. The significance of this aspect of Lesson Study will be discussed further in the section on quality Lesson Studies below.

In concluding this section, it is important to pursue the question of whether to abandon the category of MLD. The project research, taken with other evidence, raises questions about the distinctive characteristics associated with the MLD category and whether the category has significance and is useful for teaching. Although these are two important aspects of using categories like MLD, they are not the only ones. As discussed above, there is also the question of whether the category provides the grounds for allocating additional resources to some pupils seen as having additional needs. This is the administrative use of categorization; to have criteria by which to decide who receives additional resourcing. So, it can be argued that the MLD category needs to be retained for resource allocation but not for pedagogic/teaching purposes. However, it has been proposed elsewhere (Norwich, 2013b) that while some system is required to protect needed additional resource allocations, this does not have to be the traditional medically-related one. It might be one that also takes into account within-child, social and educational contexts. It could use the International Classification of Functioning (ICF) (WHO, 2002), which is a multidimensional and multidisciplinary framework. The ICF integrates the medical (focus on within pupil difficulties) and social models (focus on contextual factors), and distinguishes between impairment and the other personal and social factors that impact on activity and participation in an educational context. These conclusions point towards this kind of framework rather than just tightening up the current MLD category system. However, this would require national and international commitment to research and development work about educational classification systems along the lines of Swiss work initiated and undertaken by Hollenweger (2011); something that goes beyond the focus of this book.

Quality of Lesson Studies

A number of key points that have been underlined by the Lesson Study-MLD project are about what is involved in undertaking Lesson Studies. These are partly about the internal conditions related to undertaking Lesson Studies of what is done in Lesson Study as well as the external conditions under which Lesson Studies take place. The external conditions will be summarized and discussed in the next section. As regards the internal conditions, there are two main risks associated with Lesson Studies. One is that the basic principles and strategy of Lesson Study might not be fully understood by those engaged in the process, and so Lesson Study practice can become reduced to superficial routines. The other related risk is that parts of the Lesson Study strategy could be used selectively to make it fit current practices, perhaps because of external pressures. We have focused on Lesson Study quality in this final discussion because we recognize these risks. By quality, we mean Lesson Studies that do not involve superficial and shallow analytic approaches to understanding lesson planning, teaching and learning. However, it takes time for teachers to develop this depth of analysis, often in the early stages teachers get no further than discussing 'surface features' of a research lesson. Quality Lesson Studies involve engaging in deep analysis of teaching that is informed by relevant background knowledge and understanding and assessment of learning and learners. It reflects some of the key features of what has come to be called reflective teaching. It is notable that Lesson Study embodies most of the key features of reflective teaching as formulated by Pollard (2008). These include teaching as a cyclical process of monitoring, evaluating and revising, as competence in evidence-based classroom enquiry and as involving teacher judgement informed by research-based evidence. Reflective teaching also involves the dispositions of open-mindedness, responsibility and wholeheartedness, collaboration and dialogue with colleagues, and the creative interpretation and translation of external frameworks of teaching and learning.

At the start of the Lesson Study-MLD project, it was assumed that Lesson Study involved the following features, as explained by Pete Dudley in Chapter 2: identifying a theme/area for improvement, setting goals and research questions, having a focus on case pupils, joint planning and review that involved research lesson observation, using a trial and error process across the three research lessons, having post-lesson analysis, embodying a collaborative ethos and disseminating what has been learned. As explained in Chapter 2, the rationale for the UK version of Lesson Study, compared with other versions used internationally, is based on what this specific focus offers the lesson improvement process. Focusing on the learning of one to two pupils represents the Lesson Study priority theme. It also recognizes that pupils in any class reflect a diversity of learning characteristics and needs and enables a depth of analysis of teaching and learning in lesson observation and pupil feedback about their learning.

This was the basis of the initial model introduced to teams of teachers in the first of the two phases of the project. Through the design-based research methods, summarized in Chapter 6, we refined the initial Lesson Study strategy for teaching pupils with identified MLD. This involved introducing a more explicit preliminary review and planning team meeting before starting the first research lesson. It also led to introducing a more specific form of goal-setting for the case pupils in lesson planning that would enable goal attainment monitoring. Not only did this make it possible to assess pupils' learning gains over the period of the Lesson Studies, it also aided the Lesson Study planning process.

Another feature of Lesson Study used in the project that relates to features of Pollard's formulation of reflective teaching is the role of teacher judgement informed by research-based evidence. As shown in the model introduced in Chapter 1, the Lesson Study process was to be informed by a knowledge base that involved professional craft and research-informed knowledge. The dual and interactive use of different kinds of knowledge bases was emphasized in the Lesson Study training conferences because it has relevance to teaching pupils with learning difficulties. Analyses of the knowledge used in Lesson Studies over phases 1 and 2, which are not reported in Chapter 6, shows that Lesson Study teams did use both professional craft and research informed knowledge in their Lesson Studies. In about half of the Lesson Studies undertaken in phases 1 and 2, teachers only drew on their own professional knowledge without recourse to outside sources. In the other Lesson Studies, teachers drew on their own professional knowledge but also used some outside knowledge source. In some of these cases, there was reference to principles and practices not specifically related to learning difficulties, e.g. about how to organize cooperative group work. In other cases, there were reference principles and practices which had particular relevance to learning difficulties, e.g. working memory and thinking skills (as discussed in Chapter 3).

Lesson Study, as represented in this book, can be seen to be a version of an enquiry approach to teaching and teacher development. It is useful to be clear about the similarities and differences between Lesson Study as a general and flexible development strategy and other related approaches. Closest to Lesson Study is an approach called 'learning study'. Lesson Study and learning study both involve plan-review and collaborative aspects. Lesson Study differs in being broader in its focus on varied kinds of learning outcomes, not being confined, as is learning study, to a focus on conceptual learning using variation theory (Pang and Marton, 2003). Other kinds of enquiry approaches that are similar to Lesson Study include action research, demonstration lessons, written and/or video cases, peer observation and self-study. However, as Lewis (2009) has argued, the similarities between these approaches and Lesson Study tend to focus on one, or perhaps two aspects of Lesson Study, such as the focus on a problem in a teaching context, the observation of teaching or having shared analysis. The key difference is that Lesson Study goes beyond these other approaches by integrating a wider range of aspects (see above) that make up the specific practices, protocols and an ethos that define Lesson Study and that other approaches do not cover. This is probably best summarized by the reference to enquiry into 'lessons' in Lesson Study.

The primary and secondary Lesson Study practice case studies in Chapters 4 and 5 showed various features of lesson studies and their outcomes that correspond with the research findings, as summarized in Chapter 6. We have included these practice cases to illustrate what is involved in the Lesson Study process and to underline the importance of all the elements in process for pupils with learning difficulties. We also represent teachers' evaluations of what Lesson Study has done for them, for example, to experiment in their teaching with confidence and to focus more on pupil learning in a non-judgemental context rather than evaluating colleagues' teaching. We also report teachers' evaluations of what they gained from the process, for example, how lesson observations revealed false assumptions about pupils' responses and needs, how they identified what teaching helped or hindered learning, such as the effects of pupil grouping and the benefits of involving pupils more in their own learning. These practice cases also showed other benefits attributed to Lesson Study by these teachers, for example, how it helped to raise expectations for pupils with learning difficulties by setting learning challenges and the value of working across subject departments and collaborating with an outside specialist.

Some of these accounts are corroborated by the external evaluation research summarized in Chapter 6. For instance, outcomes attributed to Lesson Study from questionnaire and in-depth interviews revealed increased confidence in trying novel teaching approaches, more willingness to change teaching approaches, improved quality of lesson planning and increased capability to differentiate for pupils with learning difficulties than before undertaking Lesson Study. Participating teachers were also aware of the importance of the context of the Lesson Study-MLD project for the Lesson Studies they conducted. Some saw the project support as compensating for the indifference of the senior leadership in their schools. This raised questions about whether Lesson Study could be continued without project team support and the wider community of teachers established by the project. The external research also pointed to some of the key processes that might have produced these positive outcomes; feeling less threatened to scrutinize own teaching and increased interest and confidence to address SEN aspects in their subject teaching. However, this research also illustrated some of the pitfalls that arise in Lesson Studies, for example, when there is no joint but only individual esson planning and when a teacher, despite attending the training conference, continued to have misconceptions about what Lesson Study involved and could offer.

Organizational and leadership context for Lesson Study

One of the recurrent themes in both the practice case studies and the evaluation research has been the critical importance of having appropriate conditions in schools to undertake Lesson Studies and the active support of senior teachers. Lesson Study can therefore be seen to depend on the commitment to what has come to be called 'professional learning communities' in schools (Deppeler, 2012). International research about Lesson Studies has also pointed to these crucial organizational factors, as discussed above. Without the protected space and time to plan and review lessons collaboratively, Lesson Study will remain a minority activity amongst very enthusiastic teachers.

The primary teachers in the practice case studies, who were not part of the Lesson Study-MLD project, were aware that the challenge in continuing to use Lesson Study was related to organizational and cost issues. The secondary practice cases and evaluation research also showed awareness of these issues by the Lesson Study teachers. All the examples of Lesson Study in this book have been undertaken in conditions where there has been some additional funding and outside support and advice to schools. These Lesson Studies are therefore demonstration examples and may not be able to be sustained once the additional funding is removed, unless funding is extended or other funds switched to support Lesson Studies. This is where the management of professional learning in schools is crucial to embedding of Lesson Study in school systems. In an eight-months follow-up of teachers who participated in the two phases of the project, we found that teachers in about 37 per cent (or 11) of the 29 schools who completed several Lesson Studies were using or intended to continue using Lesson Studies (some teachers did not reply to our survey; this might imply that they had no intention or were not continuing with Lesson Study). There was undoubted interest and enthusiasm generated by the project in some participating teachers, and they were the ones committed to carrying on using Lesson Study. However, for others there were practical issues about when to organize the Lesson Studies without disrupting their regular class teaching.

Analysis of particular schools involved in the project showed how these organizational and management conditions operated. In one secondary school, the head teacher decided to introduce learning circles (a form of professional learning community) for most departments and make time available for teachers to collaborate with each other for professional learning purposes. Lesson Study fitted very well into this school (see Case study 2 Chapter 5). However, when the head teacher left the school, the teachers committed to Lesson Study had to then persuade the new head teacher about the benefits of continuing with this form of professional development. In another project school, the senior management were willing to continue supporting Lesson Study for those teachers interested, but not to implement it across all departments and staff. The project team also visited a school, not involved in the Lesson Study-MLD project, which had been using Lesson

Study for several years, led by the head of mathematics. In this school Lesson Study was not used in any other department.

These three examples of use of Lesson Study contrast with a particular example where the head teacher of a primary school (Case study 3) has recently developed Lesson Study across the school. In this school the main element of the school's professional development policy will be based on Lesson Study and all teachers will have an opportunity to be part of a Lesson Study group each year. These three examples also contrast with Lesson Study practice in a Singapore secondary school. This school represents the best of Singapore secondary school Lesson Study practice, which several contributors to this book visited recently. In this school, all teachers had scheduled a Lesson Study period each week before lessons started. This Singapore example gives some detail to the findings of the international report discussed above by Barber *et al.* (2010), about the role of joint planning and reviewing in professional development as a means of improving teaching and learning.

Lesson Study developments in this particular Singapore secondary school were kept separate from systems of teaching accountability and teacher performance review. This contrasts with one of the project schools (Riverside School; see Chapter 6) where a senior teacher joined the Lesson Study team and despite opposition from other team members tried to use Lesson Study for his own agenda. It emerged that his agenda was influenced by a recent Ofsted report rather than the other Lesson Study teachers' focus on learning difficulties. We also noted in our training and support work with participating teachers that some were pleasantly surprised by the Lesson Study observation focus on learning; this contrasted with the now current practice of teaching observation informed by the school inspection system operating in England. It follows that Lesson Study, with its collaborative and formative purposes, needs to be kept separate from the summative evaluation of teaching by senior management in schools.

It is clear that Lesson Study, whether applied with the aim to develop the teaching of pupils with learning difficulties or for wider teaching and learning developments, presents challenges to how schools are managed and how governments promote school development nationally. There is growing professional and research-based knowledge about how to manage schools so that they can organize and sustain the use of Lesson Study, but ultimately this requires leadership and commitment at senior teacher and national governmental levels to embed and sustain this kind of development. We met teachers on the project for whom Lesson Study reignited their passion for teaching and reminded them of why they came into teaching. It cannot be beyond the capability of governments, educational policy-makers and senior teachers to work out how to deploy a national Lesson Study strategy for the enhancement of school education for all learners.

Future prospects and ways forward

In this final section, we set out our ideas about the prospects for Lesson Study in this specific area of teaching and learning and beyond. It has emerged throughout the book that the relevance of Lesson Study to professional learning and development in the area of teaching pupils with learning difficulties cannot be separated from the wider use and conditions for Lesson Study in the school education system. So, in considering future prospects, we will briefly cover three broad interrelated aspects: (1) moderate learning difficulties/special needs and inclusive teaching, (2) Lesson Study more generally; and (3) relevant research and development approaches.

There is much scope for using and developing Lesson Study in relation to the focus of the Lesson Study-MLD project not only in secondary, but also in primary and special schools. A different approach to the one adopted in this project might be to use a Lesson Study model to focus on and apply particular research-informed approaches to teaching pupils in the spectrum of learning difficulties. This might be, for example, to apply working memory-based strategies (Gathercole and Alloway, 2008) through Lesson Study protocols in varied ways. Another example might be to focus Lesson Studies on optimizing how class teachers collaborate with teaching assistants and organize their work with pupils with learning difficulties in class teaching (Blatchford *et al.*, 2012).

Both of these research-informed examples of how to use Lesson Study also link into the use of Lesson Study beyond learning difficulties. In the dissemination of the findings and outcomes of the Lesson Study-MLD project, the project team contributed to the Department of Education's online *Advanced training materials for autism; dyslexia; speech, language and communication; emotional, social and behavioural difficulties; moderate learning difficulties* (see DfE, 2012a for these materials and programmes). This was done in two ways: the project team wrote the module on MLD but also presented a general unit about Lesson Study so that it could be used in other areas of SEN/disabilities for developing the teaching of pupils with these SEN. There is much scope for Lesson Study to be used creatively across the range of learning difficulties and disabilities.

An example of how Lesson Study can be used in a flexible and original way is its use to develop a novel classroom-based 'response to teaching' or dynamic method of assessing the learning needs of pupils who have difficulties in their learning. The idea of using Lesson Study for assessment purposes arose from informal discussions with teachers and reading their Lesson Study case reports. At the time of writing this book, there is a small-scale trial, as an extension of the Lesson Study-MLD project, in which Lesson Study teams from three primary and three secondary schools are examining how Lesson

Study can be used for assessment purposes. The key features of Lesson Study that make this possible are:

1. The collaborative model of planning, doing and reviewing short sequences of specific lessons in terms of pupil learning (three research lessons make up a Lesson Study cycle);
2. The focus on the learning of case pupils that enables a depth of assessment and analysis of pupil and learning environment (the pupil's strengths and difficulties as well as contextual supports and barriers);
3. The bringing together and integrating of different assessment perspectives and knowledge bases: from a class teacher, SEN teacher, such as a SEN coordinator, a teaching assistant as well as an outside professional, such as specialist teachers and educational psychologists; and
4. The reviewing and planning that can also take account of the pupil's perspective.

In the usual Lesson Study design as used in phases 1 and 2 of the Lesson Study-MLD project, the monitoring and review of learning, as a form of formative assessment, is used to adapt teaching, with teaching knowledge and methods as the outcome. In the assessment-driven use of Lesson Study, variations in teaching are used to derive ideas about the pupil's learning characteristics and teaching needs. Lesson Study enables a dynamic kind of assessment compared to the usual static kinds of assessment (see Chapter 3). In static assessments, the pupil performs a task unassisted and in a structured context; this performance is taken as an indicator of attainment or ability. In dynamic assessment there is monitoring of how and how well a pupil responds to the teaching of a challenging task; the dual focus is on the degree of learning gain in relation to the kinds of teaching (assistance) that support this gain. It is because of this dual focus that this kind of assessment is sometimes called a *response to teaching* model of assessment.

Dynamic or response to teaching assessment models are similar to what is called in the USA *response to instruction* (RTI) methods of assessing special educational needs (Vaughn and Fuchs, 2003). These methods assume that difficulties arise from the interaction of child and contextual factors, such as the quality of teaching and learning environment; what is also called an interactive model of learning difficulties. This model implies that assessment is not just about what a pupil can/cannot do (static assessment), but what can/cannot be done independently in response to varied and relevant teaching approaches (dynamic assessment). This has links to the Vygotskian idea of the zone of proximal development (Vygotksy, 1978), which was discussed in relation to Lesson Study in Pete Dudley's Chapter 2. What is promising about this Lesson Study approach to dynamic or response to teaching assessment is that it is curriculum-based and done during class teaching. This is unlike much dynamic assessment which has tended to focus on individual assessment of general learning and intellectual abilities (see the learning Potential Assessment Device; Feuerstein *et al.*, 1988) and been confined to individual withdrawal use by educational psychologists (Lidz and Elliott, 2000) or speech and language therapists (Hassan and Joffe, 2007).

The prospects for Lesson Study more generally are many and varied, as shown by the content of the new *International Journal of Lesson and Learning Studies*. In the Lesson Study-MLD project, one teacher transferred Lesson Study practices from the MLD project to student teachers on the PGCE programme. This proved a useful experience for the student teachers and the school continues to use Lesson Study in the PGCE school-based work. Though Lesson Study is used in several East Asian countries in initial teacher education/training, there is very little use in the UK. Lesson Study can be used to develop a coordinated system of teacher development at initial, newly qualified and continuing professional stages. It has the potential to enhance teachers' capacities at all career stages to develop and sustain more effective classroom practice. These practices have particular relevance in the current policy context in England that emphasizes school autonomy and teaching quality. Experienced teachers, school-based teacher tutors, newly qualified teachers and student teachers can work collaboratively with university tutors in Lesson Study teams. This model could also address current concerns about the role of universities in the initial and continuing professional development of teachers.

The involvement of university tutors in Lesson Studies in initial teacher education/training represents the wider question of the expertise that outside professionals can offer Lesson Studies. In Chapter 4, Gill Jordan illustrated how a reading specialist can contribute to a Lesson Study. There are examples of speech and other therapists contributing to Lesson Studies in the professional learning and training of special education teachers in Singapore (Chia and Kee, 2010). One way to ensure that Lesson Study teams have access to specialized knowledge and expertise relevant to the aims and focus of the Lesson Studies is to get outside professionals involved. This might include subject specialist and advisory teachers, therapy professions, educational psychologists and university tutors. If pupils are themselves consulted about their learning as part of the Lesson Study procedures, then it would be possible to involve parents as members of some Lesson Study teams. There is therefore also the prospect of having parents making useful contributions to Lesson Studies in early years education settings.

A final comment can also be made about the prospects of using varied research and development approaches to developing Lesson Studies. These issues were raised in Chapter 1, where we discussed the local and general route approach to improving teaching and schooling. The way in which we researched and evaluated Lesson Study in the Lesson Study-MLD project was informed by the local route approach (see Chapter 6), however, there is also some value in adopting the general route approach, perhaps using randomized control trial to experimentally evaluate Lesson Studies. If a particular use of Lesson Study is being used in an experimental evaluation, it is important to distinguish between the particular operational use of Lesson Study principles as a method and the general Lesson Study strategy. Although a particular method may be shown 'not to work', this may not reflect on the strategy, but on how it was implemented or the context of its use. The Lesson Study strategy reflects more than just techniques because it also expresses a concept of professional learning as part of a learner- and teacher-centred vision of what matters in education.

Whatever approach is adopted to researching and developing Lesson Study, there is not much that is more telling than giving excerpts from three teachers who expressed, eight months after the end of the project, what Lesson Study meant for them:

> It fuelled my passion for teaching again – I am so pleased that I took part in the project.
>
> I really hope that those higher up wake up to the missing link in the teacher training puzzle. CPD for teachers is a much poorer, staler and frankly uninspiring place without it!
>
> My whole approach to teaching and learning has changed. I am a more confident teacher.

References

AAID (American Association for Intellectual Disability) (2002) *Defintion of Mental Retardation*, www.aaidd.org, accessed 6.9.2013.

Ainscow, M. (2000) 'The next step for special education – supporting the development of inclusive practices', *British Journal of Special Education*, 27(2), 76–80.

American Psychiatric Association (2000) *Diagnostic and Statistical Manual of Mental Disorders (DSM) IV-Text Revision (2000), Mental Retardation*. Washington, DC: American Psychological Association.

Barber, M., Mourshed, M. and Chijioke, C. (2010) *How the World's Most Improved School Systems keep Getting Better*. London: McKinsey Consulting.

Bearne, E. (2004) *Raising Boys' Achievements in Literacy*. Cambridge Faculty of Education, UKLA, National Strategies, 2004, http://www.ttrb3.org.uk/wp-content/uploads/2006/12/pri_rais_boys_ach_writ_rep.pdf, accessed 21.2.2013.

Beart, S., Hardy, G.E. and Buchan, L. (2005) 'How people with intellectual disabilities view their social identity: a review of the literature', *Journal of Applied Research in Intellectual Disabilities*, 18(1), 47–56.

Ben-Hur, M. (2000) *Feuerstein's Instrumental Enrichment: Better Learning for Better Students*. New Horizons for Learning, John Hopkins University School of Education, http://education.jhu.edu/PD/newhorizons/strategies/topics/Instrumental%20Enrichment/hur.htm, accessed 12.2.2013.

Bentley, T. and Gillinson, S. (2007) *A D & R System for Education*. Innovation Unit, www.innovation-unit.co.uk, accessed 4.07.2013.

Binet, A. and Simon, T. (1905) 'Methodes nouvelles por le diagnostic du niveau intellectual des anormaux', *L'Année Psychologique*, 11, 191–244.

Blatchford, P., Russell, A. and Webster, R. (2012) *Reassessing the Impact of Teaching. Assistants: How Research Challenges Practice and Policy*. London: Routledge.

Brain Gym International (2013) *Home Page*, http://www.braingym.org, accessed 21.2.13.

Bruttin, C.D. (2011) 'Computerised assessment of an analogical reasoning test: effects of external memory strategies and their positive outcomes in young children and adolescents with intellectual disability', *Educational and Child Psychology*, 28(2), 18–32.

Burden, R. (2000) *Myself as a Leaner Scale*. Windsor: NFER-Nelson.

Campbell, F.A., Ramey, C.T., Pungello, E., Sparling, J. and Miller-Johnson, S. (2002) 'Early childhood education: young adult outcomes from the Abecedarian project', *Applied Developmental Science*, 6(1), 42–57.

Carr, W. and Kemmis, S. (1986) *Becoming Critical: Educational Knowledge and Action Research*. London: Falmer Press.

Cartwright, N.C. (2007) 'Are RCTs the gold standard?', *BioSocieties*, 2, 11–20.

Cartwright, N.C. and Stegenga, J. (2008) 'A theory of evidence for evidence-based policy'. Presented to the NRC Standing Committee on Social Science Evidence for Use, http://personal.lse.ac.uk/cartwrig/Papers%20on%20Evidence.htm, accessed 26.10.12.

Chia, N.K.W. and Kee, N.K.N. (2010) *Teaching Practicum for Special Education Teachers: A Modified Lesson Study for Trainee Special Education Teachers*. Singapore: McGraw Hill East Asia.

Clarke, A.D.B. and Clarke, A.M. (1974) 'The changing concept of intelligence: a selective historical review', in A.D.E. Clarke and A.M. Clarke (eds), *Mental Deficiency: The changing outlook*, 3rd edn, pp. 143–9. London: Methuen.

Cobb, P., Confrey, J., diSessa, A., Lehrer, R. and Schauble, L. (2003) 'Design experiments in educational research', *Educational Researcher*, 32(1), 9–13.

Cook, B.G. and Schirmer, B.R. (2003) 'What is special about special education? Overview and analysis', *The Journal of Special Education*, 37, 200–205.

Copeland, I. (2002) *The Backward Pupil over a Cycle of a Century*. Leicestershire: Upfront Publishing.

Cordingley, P., Bell, M., Rundell, B., Evans, D. and Curtis, A. (2004) *How do Collaborative and Sustained CPD and Sustained but not Collaborative CPD Affect Teaching and Learning?* London: EPPI-Centre, Institute of Education.

Crowther, D., Dyson, A. and Millward, A. (1998) *Costs and Outcomes for Pupils with Moderate Learning Difficulties in Special and Mainstream Schools*. Research Report RR89. London: DfEE.

Davis, P. and Florian, L. (2004) *Teaching Strategies and Approaches for Pupils with Special Educational Needs: A Scoping Study*. DfES Research Report RR516. London: DfES

DCSF (2009) *Lamb Enquiry Report: SEN and Parental Confidence*, DCSF 01143–2009. London: DCSF.

Deppeler, J.M. (2012) 'Developing inclusive practices: innovation through collaboration', in C. Boyle and K. Topping (eds), *What Works in Inclusion?*, pp. 125–38. Maidenhead: Open University Press.

DES (1978) *Special Educational Needs, Report of the Committee of Enquiry into the Education of Handicapped Children and Young People (The Warnock Report)*. London: HMSO.

Desforges, C.W. (2004) 'Collaboration: why bother?' *Nexus*, 3, 6–7.

Detterman, D.K., Gabriel, L.T. and Ruthsatz, J.M. (2000) 'Intelligence and mental retardation', in Sternberg (ed.) *Handbook of Intelligence*, pp. 141–58. Cambridge: Cambridge University Press.

DfE (2011a) *Achievement for All Evaluation: Final report*. DFE-RR171. London: DFE.

DfE (2011b) *Children with Special Educational Needs 2011: An Analysis – Chapter 1 Tables*. London: DfE.

DfE (2011c) *Support and Aspiration: A New Approach to Special Educational Needs and Disability*. London: HMSO.

DfE (2012a) *Advanced Training Materials For Autism; Dyslexia; Speech, Language And Communication; Emotional, Social And Behavioural Difficulties; Moderate Learning Difficulties*. http://www.education.gov.uk/lamb/resources/SpLD/Unit%20PDFs/9_lesson_study.pdf and http://www.education.gov.uk/lamb/module4/M04U09.html?s=1, accessed 23.3.2013.

DfE (2012b) *SEN in England, January 2012, Statistical First Release*. London: DFE.

DfES (2001) *Special Educational Needs Code of Practice*. London: DfES.

DfES (2003) *Data Collection by Type of Special Educational Needs*. London: DfES.

Dudley, P. (2004) 'Lessons for learning: research lesson study, innovation, transfer and meta-pedagogy; a design experiment?' Paper presented at the Fifth Annual Conference of the TLRP, 22–24 November, Cardiff, Wales.

Dudley, P. (2005) *Summary report of the Lesson Study Pilot for the CfBT board and the Teaching and Learning Research Programme*. Unpublished report.

Dudley, P. (2007) 'The lesson study model of classroom enquiry', *Teaching and Leaning Update*. London: Optimus.

Dudley, P. (2008) 'Lesson study in England'. Paper presented at the World Association of Lesson Studies Annual Conference, Hong Kong Institute of Education, December 2008.

Dudley, P. (2011) Lessons for Learning: How Teachers Learn in Contexts of Lesson Study. Unpublished doctoral thesis, University of Cambridge.

Dudley, P. (2012) 'Lesson study development in England: from school networks to national policy', *International Journal for Lesson and Learning Studies*, 1(1), 85–100.

Dudley, P. (2013) 'Teacher learning in lesson study: what interaction-level discourse analysis revealed about how teachers utilised imagination, tacit knowledge of teaching and freshly gathered evidence of pupils learning, to develop their practice knowledge and so enhance their pupils' learning', *Teaching and Teacher Education* 34(107), 221.

Dunsmuir, S., Brown, E., Iyadurai, S. and Monsen, J. (2009) 'Evidence?based practice and evaluation: from insight to impact', *Educational Psychology in Practice*, 25(1), 54–70.

Elliott, J. (1991) *Action Research for Educational Change*. Buckingham: Open University Press.

Elliott, J.G. and Gibbs, S. (2009) 'Does dyslexia exist?', *Journal of Philosophy of Education*, 42(3–4), 475–91.

Feuerstein, R., Rand, Y. and Rynders, J.E. (1988) *Don't Accept me as I am: Helping 'Retarded' People to Excel*. New York: Plenum Press.

Fisher, R. (2006) 'Thinking skills', in J. Arthur, T. Grainger and D. Wray (eds), *Learning to Teach in Primary School*, pp. 56–67. London: Routledge Falmer.

Fletcher-Campbell, F. (2004) 'Moderate learning difficulties', in A. Lewis and B. Norwich (eds), *Special Teaching for Special Children? Pedagogies for Inclusion*, pp. 354–366. Maidenhead: Open University Press.

Florian, L. (2010) 'Special education in an era of inclusion: the end of special education or a new beginning?', *The Psychology of Education Review*, 34(2), 22–9.

Frederickson, N. and Cline. T. (2009) *Special Educational Needs, Inclusion and Diversity*. Maidenhead: McGraw Hill.

Gallimore, R., and Stigler, J. (2003) 'Closing the teaching gap: assisting teachers to adapt to change', in C. Richardson (ed.), *Whither Assessment*, pp. 25–36. London: Qualifications and Curriculum Authority.

Gathercole, S.E. and Alloway, T.P. (2008) *Working Memory and Learning: A Practical Guide for Teachers*. London: Sage.

Goffman, E. (1963) *Stigma: Notes on the Management of Spoiled Identity*. Englewood Cliffs, NJ: Prentice Hall.

Goleman, D. (1995) *Emotional Intelligence*. New York: Bantam.

Guskey, T.R. (2002) 'Professional development and teacher change', *Teachers and Teaching: Theory and Practice*, 8(3), 9–38.

Hadfield, M., Jopling, M. and Emira, M. (2011) *Evaluation of the National Strategies' Primary Leading Teachers Programme*. Wolverhampton: University of Wolverhampton.

Hammersley, M. (2007) *Educational Research and Evidence-based Practice*. London: Sage.

Hart, L.C., Alston, A.S. and Murata, A. (eds) (2011) *Lesson Study Research and Practice in Mathematics Education: Learning Together*. London: Springer.

Hassan, N. and Joffe, V. (2007) 'The case for dynamic assessment in speech and language therapy', *Child Language Teaching and Therapy*, 23(1), 9–25.

Hollenweger, J. (2011) 'Development of an ICF-based eligibility procedure for education in Switzerland', *BMC Public Health*, 11(Supplement 5), 1–8.

Houston, G. (1984) *Red Book of Groups: And How to Lead them Better*. New York: John Wiley.

Howes, A.J., Davies, S.M.B. and Fox, S. (2009) *Improving the Context for Inclusion: Personalising Teacher Development through Collaborative Action Research*. London: Routledge.

Jeffries, S. and Everatt, J. (2004) 'Working memory: its role in dyslexia and other specific learning difficulties', *Dyslexia*, 10, 196–214.

Jones, M.C., Walley, R.M., Leech, A., Paterson, M., Common, S. and Metcalf, C. (2006) 'Using goal attainment scaling to evaluate a needs-led exercise programme for people with severe and profound intellectual disabilities', *Journal of Intellectual Disabilities*, 10(4), 317–35.

Jusin, L. and Harber, K.D. (2005) 'Teacher expectations and self-fulfilling prophecies: knowns and unknowns, resolved and unresolved controversies', *Personality and Social Psychology Review*, 9(2), 131–55.

Kagan, S. (1989) *Think Pair Share Strategy*, http://literacy.purduecal.edu/STUDENT/ammessme/ThinkPairShare.html, accessed 21. 2. 2013.

Ko, Po Yuk. (2012) 'Critical conditions for pre-service teachers' learning through inquiry: The Learning Study approach in Hong Kong', *International Journal for Lesson and Learning Studies*, 1(1), 49–64.

Kofler, M.J., Rapport, M.D., Bolden, J. and Altro, T.A. (2008) *Working Memory as a Core Deficit in ADHD: Preliminary Findings and Implications. The ADHD Report*. Guilford Press, http://clclinic.cos.ucf.edu/Documents%20and%20Files/adhd.2008.16.6.pdf, accessed 31. 01. 2013.

Kozulin, A., Lebeer, J., Madella-Noja, A. Gonzalez, F., Jeffrey, I., Rosenthal, N. and Koslowsky, M. (2010) 'Cognitive modifiability of children with developmental disabilities: A multicentre study using Feuerstein's Instrumental Enrichment-Basic program', *Research in Developmental Disabilities*, 31(2), 551–9.

Lee, J.F.K. (2008) 'A Hong Kong case of Lesson Study – benefits and concerns', *Teaching and Teacher Education*, 24(5), 1115–24.

Lewis, A. and Norwich, B. (2005) *Special Teaching for Special Children? Pedagogies for inclusion*. Maidenhead: Open University Press.

Lewis, C. (1998) 'A lesson is like a swiftly flowing river: how research lessons improve Japanese education', *American Educator*, (Winter), 12–17 and 50–51.

Lewis, C. (2009) 'What is the nature of knowledge development in lesson study?', *Educational Action Research*, 17(1), 95–110.

Lewis, C., Perry, R. and Murata, A. (2006) 'How should research contribute to instructional improvement? The case of lesson study', *Educational Researcher*, 35(3), 3–14.

Lewis, C., Perry, R.R. and Hurd, J. (2009) 'Improving mathematics instruction through lesson study: a theoretical model and North American case', *Journal of Mathematics Teacher Education*, 12, 285–304.

Lidz, C. and Elliott, J.G. (2000) *Dynamic Assessment: Prevailing Models and Applications*. New York: JAI Press.

Lieberman, J. (2009) 'Reinventing teacher professional norms and identities: the role of lesson study and learning communities', *Professional Development in Education*, 35(1), 83–99.

Lim, C., Lee, C., Saito, E. and Haron, S.S. (2011) 'Taking stock of Lesson Study as a platform for teacher development in Singapore', *Asia-Pacific Journal of Teacher Education*, 39(4), 353–65.

Lo, M. and Marton, F. (2012) 'Towards a science of the art of teaching: using variation theory as a guiding principle of pedagogical design', *International Journal of Learning and Lesson Studies*, 1(1), 7–22.

Lo, M.L. and Ko, P.Y. (2002) 'The enacted object of learning', in F. Marton and P. Morris (eds), *What Matters? Discovering Critical Conditions for Classroom Learning*, pp. 59–73. Goteborg: Acta Universitatis Gothoburgensis.

MacMillan, D., Siperstein, G.N. and Gresham, F.M. (1996) 'A challenge to the viability of mild mental retardation as a diagnostic category', *Exceptional Children*, 62(4), 356–71.

Miles, S., and Ainscow, M. (2011) *Responding to Diversity: An Inquiry-based Approach*. London: Routledge.

NCSL (National College for School Leadership) (2005) *Getting Started with Networked Lesson Study*. Nottingham, NCSL/CfBT.

National Strategies/DCSF (2002) *Creative Thinking in Literacy, Art and Design*. http://www.teachingexpertise.com/resources/creative-thinking-literacy-art-and-design–3592, accessed 21.2.13.

Norwich, B. (2013a) *Addressing Tensions and Dilemmas in Inclusive Education*. Abingdon: Routledge.

Norwich, B. (2013b) 'Categories of special educational needs', in L. Florian (ed.), *Sage Handbook of SEN*, 2nd edn, pp. 55–66. London: Sage.

Norwich, B. and Kelly, N. (2005) *Moderate Learning Difficulties and the Future of Inclusion*. London: RoutlegeFalmer.

Norwich, B. and Lewis, A. (2005) 'How specialised is teaching children with difficulties and disabilities?', in A. Lewis and B. Norwich (eds), *Special Teaching for Special Children? Pedagogies for inclusion*, pp. 1–11. Maidenhead: Open University Press.

Norwich, B., Ylonen, A. and Gwernan-Jones, R. (2012) 'Moderate learning difficulties – searching for clarity and understanding', *Research Papers in Education*, doi: 10.1002/dys.278.

Nuthall, G. and Alton-Lee, A. (1993) 'Predicting learning from student experience of teaching: a theory of student knowledge construction in classrooms', *American Educational Research Journal*, 30(4), 799–840.

Ofsted (2010) *The Special Educational Needs and Disability Review: A Statement is Not Enough.* London: HMSO.
Opfer, V.D. and Pedder, D. (2010) 'Benefits, status and effectiveness of continuous professional development for teachers in England', *The Curriculum Journal*, 21(4), 413–31.
Pang, M. and Marton, F. (2003) 'Beyond "Lesson Study": comparing two ways of facilitating the grasp of some economic concepts', *Instructional Science*, 31, 175–94.
Pawson, R. and Tilley, N. (1997) *Realistic Evaluation.* London: SAGE.
Pedder, D. (2006) 'Organisational conditions that foster successful classroom promotion of learning how to learn', *Research Papers in Education*, 21(2), 171–200.
Pedder, D., Opfer, D., McCormick, R. and Storey, A. (2010) 'Schools and continuing professional development in England – 'State of the Nation' research study: policy, context, aims and design', *Curriculum Journal*, 21(4), 365–94.
Perry, R.R. and Lewis, C.C. (2009) 'What is successful adaptation of lesson study in the US?', *Journal of Educational Change*, 10, 365–91.
Pollard, I. (2008) *Reflective Teaching*, 3rd edn. London: Continuum Publishers.
Prince-Embury, S. (2007) *Resiliency Scales for Children and Adolescents: A Profile of Personal Strengths.* San Antonio, TX: Pearson.
Puchner, L.D. and Taylor, A.R. (2006) 'Lesson study, collaboration and teacher efficacy: stories from two school-based math lesson study groups', *Teaching and Teacher Education*, 22(7), 922–34.
Quirk, M.P. and Schwanenflugel, P.J. (2004) 'Do supplemental remedial reading programs address the motivational issues of struggling readers? An analysis of five popular programs', *Reading Research and Instruction*, 43(3), 1–19.
Raison, G. (2013) *Cooperative Reading as Simple as ABC*, http://www.cdesign.com.au/proceedings_aate/aate_papers/028_raison.htm, accessed 21.2.2013.
Ramey, C.T. and Campbell, F.A. (1992) 'Poverty, early childhood education, and academic competence: The Abecedarian experiment', in A. Huston (ed.), *Children in Poverty*, pp. 190–221. New York: Cambridge University Press.
RCBDD (Royal Commission on the Blind, the Deaf and Dumb), (1889) *Report Volume IV.* London: HMSO.
Rix, J., Hall, K., Nind, M., Sheehy, K. and Wearmouth, J. (2009) 'What pedagogical approaches can effectively include children with special educational needs in mainstream classrooms? A systematic literature review', *Support for Learning*, 24(2), 86–96.
Robinson, V., Hohepa, M. and Lloyd, C. (2009) *School Leadership and Student Outcomes: Identifying What Works and Why Best Evidence Synthesis.* Auckland: New Zealand Ministry of Education.
Rock, T. and Wilson, C. (2005) 'Improving teaching through lesson study', *Teacher Education Quarterly*, 32(1), 77–92.
Rosenthal, R. and Jacobson, L.F. (1968) 'Teacher expectations for the disadvantaged', *Scientific American*, 218(4), 19–23.
Runesson, U. and Gustafsson, G. (2012) 'Sharing and developing knowledge products from learning study', *International Journal for Lesson and Learning Studies*, 1(3), 245–60.

Sibbald, T. (2009) 'The relationship between lesson study and self-efficacy', *School Science and Mathematics*, 109(8), 450–60.

Sims, L. and Walsh, D. (2009) Lesson study with preservice teachers: lessons from lessons', *Teaching and Teacher Education*, 25(5), 724–33.

Stigler, J. and Hiebert, J. (1999) *The Teaching Gap*. New York: Free Press.

Takahashi, A. (2005) 'An essential component of lesson study: post-lesson discussion'. Paper presented at the Northwest Regional Educational Laboratory's Lesson Study Symposium, Olympia, Washington: DePaul University, Chicago.

TDA (2009) *Removing Barriers: MLD. Training toolkit*. London: TDA.

Van der Molen, M.J., Van Luit, J.E.H., Johgmans, M.J. and Van der Molen, M.W. (2007) 'Verbal working memory in children with mild intellectual disabilities', *Journal of Intellectual Disability Research*, 51(2), 162–9.

Vaughn, S. and Fuchs, L.S. (2003) 'Redefining learning disabilities as inadequate response to instruction: the promise and potential problems', *Learning Disability Research and Practice*, 18(3), 137–46.

Vygotksy, L. (1978) *Mind in Society: The Development of Higher Psychological Processes*. Cambridge, MA: Harvard University Press.

Watanabe, T. (2002) 'Learning from Japanese lesson study', *Education Leadership*, 59(6), 36–9.

Wertsch, J.V. (1981) *The Concept of Activity in Soviet Psychology*. Armonk, NY: Sharpe.

WHO (2002) *International Classification of Functioning, Disability and Health: Towards a Common Language for Functioning, Disability and Health*. Geneva: WHO.

Willis, S. (2002) 'Creating a knowledge base for teaching: a conversation with James Stigler', *Educational Leadership*, 59(6), 6–11.

Yeo, D. (2003) *Dyslexia Dyspraxia and Mathematics*. London: Whurr.

Ylonen, A. and Norwich, B. (2012) 'Using lesson study to develop teaching approaches for secondary school pupils with moderate learning difficulties: teachers' concepts, attitudes and pedagogic strategies', *European Journal of Special Needs Education*, 27(3), 301–17.

Ylonen, A. and Norwich, B. (2013) 'Professional learning of teachers through a lesson study process: contexts, mechanisms and outcomes', *International Journal of Lesson and Learning Studies*, 2(2), 137–54.

Yoshida, M. (2012) 'Mathematics lesson study in the United States – current status and ideas for conducting high quality and effective lesson study', *International Journal for Lesson and Learning Studies*, 1(2), 140–52.

Index